Elizabeth Cady Stanton
A Radical for Woman's Rights

OTHER BOOKS BY LOIS W. BANNER

Women in Modern America: A Brief History
Clio's Consciousness Raised: New Perspectives on the
History of Women (with Mary S. Hartman),
anthology

Lois W. Banner

Elizabeth Cady Stanton
A Radical for Woman's Rights

Edited by Oscar Handlin

Little, Brown and Company · Boston · Toronto

79-4291

Library of Congress Catalog Card No. 79-2242
Second Printing

Frontispiece and illustration facing page 1 courtesy of Brown Brothers, Sterling, Pennsylvania 18463.

Published simultaneously in Canada
by Little, Brown & Company (Canada) Limited

PRINTED IN THE UNITED STATES OF AMERICA

For Gideon and Olivia,
and especially to Jim

Editor's Preface

THE REFORM movements that took shape in the 1830s attacked a variety of problems, all of which seemed impediments to improvement of the common man. Each benevolent band addressed a specific evil, seeking to eliminate slavery, intemperance, insanity, and poverty in order to raise the general level of humanity. All, however, embraced an impulse toward perfectionism. Since progress was inevitable and since a divine spark nestled within each human consciousness, nothing more was necessary to correct apparent social disorders than to remove the outmoded obstacles inherited from the past.

Inevitably, in this process some Americans wondered, why just men and not women also? Disabilities based on sex seemed also to be anachronisms, survivals of ancient prejudice. Females, like males, were susceptible to improvement if only they were liberated. The calls for equality echoed and reinforced suggestions of feminism that had been sounded in the New World since the eighteenth century. They now became louder, more affirmative and more difficult to set aside.

Elizabeth Cady Stanton was born in the Burned Over district of New York, long a center of the reform activity. Early on, family connections and her own lively intellectual curiosity made her a participant in these movements. A long life brought her through the Civil War, through national expansion and industrialization, and on into the complex culture of the United States at the end of the nineteenth century.

Through the profound changes in the lives of American women as in the condition of their country, she bore a vision of liberation that she expressed in a unique vigorous fashion, constantly exploring its implications.

Yet she was far from being a fanatical reformer. A warm, fun loving woman, Elizabeth Cady Stanton led a full life, the zest of which permitted her to apply herself enthusiastically in pursuit of her goals. Lois Banner's lively account of the woman and the campaigns that enlisted her support throws light on many aspects of the development of American society.

OSCAR HANDLIN

Acknowledgments and Notes

IN PREPARING this manuscript, I wish to acknowledge the inestimable aid of Rhoda Barney Jenkins, daughter of Nora Blatch Barney, granddaughter of Harriot Stanton Blatch, and great-granddaughter of Elizabeth Cady Stanton. Among other help, Ms. Jenkins provided information about Cady Stanton's health and described to me the family legend regarding Cady Stanton's death. Most important, she shared with me the Cady-Stanton-Blatch family genealogy, which is in her possession, and from which I was able to reconstruct the details of the Cady births and deaths contained in Chapter One. I also wish to acknowledge the help of George T. Engelman, Jr., president of the Johnstown Historical Society, who checked Cady genealogical information for me in the Johnstown cemetery records, and of Virginia Moseley, Tenafly borough historian, and Joyce Herman, owner of the Tenafly Cady Stanton house, who told me much about the town and Cady Stanton's years there.

Among the staffs of the many libraries who helped me in securing Cady Stanton's letters and other manuscripts, I would like to thank in particular the staff members of the Douglass College Library of Rutgers University, who assisted me in using the Theodore Stanton Collection, which no Cady Stanton scholar has yet examined.

I would like to thank the following for permission to reprint copyrighted or previously unpublished material:

The Mabel Smith Douglass Library, Rutgers University Libraries, New Brunswick, New Jersey, for numerous quotations from material in the Theodore Stanton Collection.

The Vassar College Library, for quotations from the Elizabeth Cady Stanton Papers.

The Schlesinger Library, Radcliffe College, for quotations from the Blackwell Papers, Olympia Brown Papers, and Harriet Robinson Papers.

The Sophia Smith Collection (Women's History Archive), Smith College, for quotations from the Garrison Family Papers.

The Department of Rare Books, Manuscripts and Archives, University of Rochester Library, for a quotation from a Stanton manuscript in their collections.

The George Arents Library for Special Collections at Syracuse University, Syracuse, New York, for quotations from materials in the Gerrit Smith Collection.

The Seneca Falls Historical Society, Seneca Falls, New York, for Cady Stanton's blessing at mealtime, which appears in a Margaret Stanton Lawrence manuscript letter in their collection.

The Minnesota Historical Society, for a quotation from "Reminiscences of Elizabeth Cady Stanton" in the Political Equality Club of Minnesota Papers.

The Missouri Historical Society, St. Louis, Missouri, for a quotation from a letter in the Lillie Devereux Blake Collection.

Harper & Row, Publishers, for numerous small quotations from *Elizabeth Cady Stanton as Revealed in Her Letters, Diary, and Reminiscences,* edited by Theodore Stanton and Harriot Stanton Blatch.

Rhoda Barney Jenkins and John Barney, for permission to quote from all of their great-grandmother's unpublished writings.

I would also like to thank those individuals whose critical readings of the manuscript were of invaluable aid: Anne Firor Scott, James McLachlan, Mary Kelley, Bertram Wyatt-Brown, James M. Banner, Jr., and Oscar Handlin. I am indebted to Judith Walkowitz for sharing with me material on late nineteenth-century English feminists from her forthcoming study of English prostitution and the English moral reform movement.

I have chosen to call the subject of my study during the period of her childhood and youth Elizabeth Cady or, more simply, Elizabeth. Beginning with her marriage in 1840, and symbolic of her growing feminism and maturity, I refer to her as Cady Stanton. This was, in fact, the name she chose for herself at the time of her marriage and used for the rest of her life. Also, although the term "feminism" was not coined until the late nineteenth century, for stylistic reasons and because of its common usage I have employed the expression interchangeably with the nineteenth-century variant, woman's rights, to refer to the advocacy of equal rights for women.

Because this book is based substantially on primary sources which scholars have not yet utilized, I have deposited a footnoted typescript copy at the Elizabeth Bancroft Schlesinger Library, Radcliffe College.

Contents

Elizabeth Cady Stanton

A Radical for Woman's Rights

I

A Time of Choice:
Johnstown and Peterboro

IN ELIZABETH CADY'S childhood two influences predominated: first, the conservative family and community of Johnstown, New York, in which she was born and raised; second, the liberal and reformist family of her cousin, Gerrit Smith, of Peterboro, New York. As a child and young woman, she revealed two sides of a complex personality. Outwardly she seemed a carefree tomboy, with social grace and native wit, the natural leader of any group, the life of any gathering. Privately, however, she was often morbidly introspective, afraid of death, and prone to nightmares, depressions, and rages. How to integrate the disparate elements of her personality was the central dilemma of her early life.

Elizabeth Cady's roots lay in the well-to-do, ruling classes of New York. Through her mother, Margaret Livingston Cady, she was related to the oldest and wealthiest families of the state —the Beekmans, the Schuylers, the Van Rensselaers, and, especially, the Livingstons. Through shrewd land dealings and marriages, Livingston forebears had carved out baronial estates on the Hudson. They were leaders of the political, social, and business life of New York throughout the first decades of the nineteenth century. Elizabeth's maternal grandfather, James Livingston, belonged to a collateral branch of the main family, and his fortune was not vast. But he had been a member of the state assembly and of the first board of regents of the state university and, like numerous Livingston men, had served with distinction in the revolutionary army.

Daniel Cady, Elizabeth's father, was a prominent lawyer of humble origins. Son of a farmer, he had worked as a blacksmith before studying with an Albany lawyer and establishing his own practice in Johnstown. He quickly gained a reputation for expertise in land law and courtroom pleading. Marriage to an Albany Livingston in 1801 was testimony to his success. He served in the New York Assembly during several sessions and for one term in the national House of Representatives. In 1847 he became a justice of the New York State Supreme Court.

In their personal and political beliefs, Elizabeth Cady's parents were conservatives. Daniel Cady was a staunch Federalist. Like many self-made men, he identified with his new status and his wife's patrician values. He believed in the sanctity of the law and of private property. He thought that the United States offered an equal opportunity to everyone and that his own success was proof of his native ability and, by implication, of the native ability of all those who had similarly succeeded. But he was not without charity. He shared the Federalist sentiment that the wealthy and powerful had a responsibility to exercise control wisely and in the best interests of society and as a lawyer and jurist won renown for fairness and personal integrity.

The conservatism of Elizabeth Cady's parents was reflected in their method of raising their children. Aristocratic Livingston values were apparent in their fine house, their servants, and their stable of horses. Margaret Livingston Cady carefully trained her daughters in the genteel domestic arts appropriate to future wives of the gentry. But the household emphasized duty, submission, and order above all. The children were supposed to regard their parents, and all adults in authority, with fear and respect. Self-control, not independence, was the desired end. Time was regimented, and loud, boisterous behavior indoors was not tolerated. Aside from the servants, the family was nuclear: neither grandparents nor aunts and uncles lived in the house. Of the ten children born to the Cadys, six survived early childhood. These included Elizabeth's older brother Eleazer, her older sisters Tryphena and Harriet, and her younger sisters Margaret and Katherine.

The family's religion was old school Presbyterianism. By 1815 most traditional American denominations, threatened by the advance of secularism and the fast growing Methodist and Baptist churches, had made their doctrines more appealing by softening Calvinist notions of predestination and human depravity and by introducing revivals. Old school Presbyterians, however, had introduced few innovations. They frowned on revivals and continued to follow a strict form of Calvinism which attracted the conservative barrister and his wife, proud of a Livingston ancestry which had originated in Scotland, the birthplace of Calvinist Presbyterianism. In Johnstown, Cady Stanton remembered, religion was omnipresent. The church bell continually rang, for school, church, prayer meetings, and, above all, she recalled, for funerals.

Her parents' child rearing practices and their religion stimulated in the sensitive Elizabeth Cady what the twentieth century might call neurosis. She had recurrent nightmares about funerals, with bodies in black, mourners in crepe, and ministers ranting over the misdeeds of the living and the dead. At one point she imagined that she was a secret child of the devil, who was bent on claiming her. Under the spell of this dread, for many nights she shivered in secret on the stairs, where the hall lamps of her home and the sound of adult voices were comforting. She developed a fear of her surroundings and regarded Johnstown as a community steeped in violence and not as a bucolic farming center. Its founder, Sir William Johnson, had been a central figure in the decades of bloody wars in the Mohawk Valley among the French, the English, and the Indians. Johnson's manor house, "gloomy and threatening" to the young girl, still stood, with "the marks of the Indian's tomahawk on the balustrades" and the stories of "the bloody deeds there enacted." Even her immediate environment seemed threatening. From the poplar trees which lined the main streets of Johnstown dangled small yellow inch worms which terrified the child.

When depressed Elizabeth would simply go to sleep. Frequently she fell into hysterical rages. Such behavior was partly the expression of a dramatic personality, whose youthful emotionalism would later translate into a brilliant oratorical ability and platform style. But the fantasies, the depressions, and the anger also reflected a deep-seated sense of guilt and rejection. Elizabeth clearly felt a lack of love, and it is equally clear that she judged her mother the primary culprit. Autobiographical accounts of her childhood consistently held her mother responsible for the harsh family discipline. She characterized Margaret Cady as an aristocratic Livingston who could not handle her volatile fifth child, who paid little attention to Elizabeth's love of learning, and was primarily interested that her daughters learn domestic arts and genteel skills. That her mother was nearly six feet tall—an extraordinary height for a woman of that age—must have intensified her intimidating character to Elizabeth Cady, who was a small child and a short woman.

In her own right, Margaret Cady was complex. She was by others' accounts beautiful and witty, with great social presence. Harriot Stanton Blatch, Elizabeth Cady Stanton's daughter, adored her maternal grandmother. Blatch's description of Margaret Cady as a warm and natural confidante of children with great skill in personal relationships was in direct contrast to her mother's characterization. Blatch realized that Margaret Cady was married to an older man who was absorbed in his work and often absent at sessions of the state legislature or the circuit courts. Her grandmother, Blatch contended, kept the family together. It was she who insisted that the family live in the center of Johnstown, in the midst of town society, rather than on one of the farms Daniel Cady owned in the countryside. And although her husband often scorned the domestic skills she taught their daughters, she wanted the girls prepared for possible marriage outside the elite.

Moreover, Margaret Cady's marriage was tinged with a tragedy that affected the rest of the family and contributed to Elizabeth Cady's own feelings of guilt and rejection. Margaret Livingston married Daniel Cady in 1801, when she was only sixteen and he, at twenty-eight, was twelve years older. Children quickly followed. By the time Elizabeth was born in 1815, her mother had borne six children—enough pregnancies under any circumstances to be a severe emotional and physical drain. Of these six children, three had died—a family mortality rate not unusual in an age of primitive medicine and rampant disease. Yet what shattered the family was that, of the three sons born during these years, two had died. Daniel Cady in particular experienced "an agony of suffering" which "half carried him from life" when his namesake Daniel died in 1814 at the age of seven. Of the male children, only eight-year-old Eleazer then remained.

Margaret and Daniel Cady preferred male children to female, particularly since Livingston family fortunes had been based partly on producing many sons. Nineteenth-century parents of their class expected that sons would distinguish themselves in business, politics, or the professions and would thereby preserve the family reputation and carry on the line. Daughters were another matter. Barred from college educations and the professions, regarded in theology, law, and philosophy as subordinate, daughters were expected simply to marry and to merge themselves in their families, altogether obedient to their husbands. In musing on the genesis of her feminism, Cady Stanton later asserted that her first conscious childhood memory was of adult visitors commiserating with her parents on the birth of her young sister, Katherine, in 1820.

The Cady family tragedy continued. In 1826 Eleazer, a gifted youth and the last of the Cady boys, died, two months after graduating from Union College in nearby Schenectady. Daniel Cady broke down completely. Margaret Cady, in contrast, exhibited extraordinary strength. In 1827 she bore another son, even though for seven years she had had no children—mute testimony to her own difficulties over earlier births and child rearing and evidence that she probably used some form of birth control, probably abstinence. This son, following contemporary practice, was named Eleazer after his older brother. He was obviously seen as his late brother's replacement, although he died in 1829. Then forty-four, Margaret Livingston was approaching menopause, the mother of five daughters and no sons. Apparently suffering some sort of breakdown, she gave the household management over to her grown daughter and son-in-law, Tryphena and Edward Bayard, who lived with the family.

Partly in compensation for what she felt as maternal rejection, Elizabeth formed other supportive bonds. The family's black servant, Peter Teabout, warm and loving, for many years watched the younger girls and gained their confidence by taking them on exciting visits to the courthouse and the jail across the town square from their home and by rarely reporting misdeeds to their parents. In her mature years Cady Stanton traced her interest in the law and in prison reform partly to these visits, where she listened to lawyers pleading their cases and heard the prisoners' stories. Witnessing prejudice against Peter predisposed her toward her later abolitionism. In addition, the family pastor, the Reverend Simon Hosack, expounder of conservative theology, was responsive to Elizabeth's needs. Without children of his own, he took to heart the bright young girl, encouraged her ambitions, and for many years tutored her in Greek at her request. His church and rectory were close to the Cady house; and he often let her drive him on his rounds while he read *Blackwell's Magazine* or *The Edinburgh Review* aloud to her and patiently explained the meaning of complex ideas. For Elizabeth's often absent father, he was a substitute; his love and esteem bolstered her own self-respect. When he died he willed her the Greek lexicon, grammar, and testament that he had used since his student days.

Elizabeth Cady also gained a strengthened sense of identity from growing up with four sisters and only one brother, who was much older. Despite the favoritism accorded Eleazer and the training in domesticity her mother enforced, Elizabeth could retreat to the community of women her sisters constituted in order to reinforce her sense of self-worth. Harriet and Margaret, nearest her in age, disliked the strict family regimen as much as Elizabeth herself. The three of them forged a confederacy in rebellion, acting on Margaret's suggestion that they defy the "everlasting no" from their parents and do what they wanted. Harriet was a sickly child, often confined to the house, and Margaret was younger. Given her vitality and force, Elizabeth emerged as their leader.

Alienated from her mother, Elizabeth Cady also looked to her father for support. Most people found Daniel Cady stern and severe. To Elizabeth, he seemed shy and sensitive and sympathetic to her desire to escape maternal discipline and training in domesticity. Her father, she recalled, had a childish love of fun and fresh air. She speculated that his example "had quite as much to do with our rebellion against maternal authority as our own natural proclivities." The mature Cady Stanton remembered that her father upheld her in her periodic rebellions against hated sewing sessions. He was proud of her eventual skill at horsemanship, and if he saw her sewing he would tell her to go riding and let a servant—"a good strong Irish girl"—do the work. And there was an adventurous strain in his character. When a young lawyer he had ridden the court circuit in the near wilderness of upstate New York; he had settled in Johnstown when the area was little more than frontier. He told tales of adventures with Indians and frontiersmen, of court sessions in log cabins, and of nights spent camping on floors with judges, juries, sheriffs, and defendants.

When an exasperated Margaret Livingston sent the rebellious Elizabeth for discipline to her father in his law office, he would usually simply let her listen to his discussions with his clients or read the volumes in the bookshelves along the walls —activities which she loved. In such reading and listening she gained her first knowledge of her society's discrimination against women. One case in particular she never forgot. Flora

Campbell, an old family servant who supplied the Cadys with farm produce, sought to recover a farm, purchased with her money, which her deceased husband had willed to their improvident son. Cady explained that he could do nothing, and he showed Campbell the laws which made a woman's possessions the property of her husband when they married. The law of most states then defined married women as extensions of their husband's persons and possessions and gave husbands full rights over their wives' property, earnings, and children. Because they were considered legally indistinct from their husbands, wives could not testify against husbands in court and were subject to moderate corporal punishment by them.

Distressed by Flora Campbell's case as well as by the general legal inequality of women, Elizabeth resolved to cut the offending discriminatory passages from her father's law books with a knife. Discovering her intent, Daniel Cady explained that laws were much more than just words in legal digests in his office. The mature Elizabeth remembered that, to soothe her, he suggested that she could perhaps work to change the laws when she grew up.

It is improbable that Daniel Cady ever made such a suggestion. But he seemed to approve, however inadvertently, Elizabeth's youthful outrage against woman's lot and thereby supported the genesis of her feminism. Elizabeth was his favorite daughter. He liked her independence and respected her intelligence. He encouraged her to study the law and when she was older occasionally took her with him to Albany or on the circuit as a legal assistant. Cady Stanton later went to great lengths to identify with her father; she even contended that she had inherited her ease in falling asleep from him. It was not just his influence and reputation that attracted her; his gentle, rebellious, playful side was equally important. She early defined him as the person she wanted to become—a person who combined gentleness with power and who had, by dint of his own efforts, become a considerable success.

Growing up in Johnstown also gave Elizabeth Cady certain advantages. In that town of 1,000 inhabitants, society was relatively unstructured; she played freely with the village boys in their rough and tumble games and competed with them in school. Johnstown was a stopover on the main East-West road and was celebrated for its hotels. The county courthouse was located across from the Cady home, on the edge of the town square, and many eminent lawyers pleaded cases there. They often came to dinner at the Cady home and were entertained by Elizabeth's legal learning. As his renown grew, Daniel Cady increasingly attracted young men as law students. Often boarding with the Cadys and present in the attorney's law office, which was adjacent to the house, they flirted with the Cady daughters and teased Elizabeth about women's legal subordination. Their bantering heightened her sensitivity to the issue. Elizabeth could also go to the court, the jail, or to her father's office with ease and was spared the isolation of the farm and the restricted residential areas of the great cities, where propriety barred women from courthouses and business districts.

Cady Stanton retained a deep affection for her family and for the community of her youth. In later years, with a growing family of her own, a husband often away, and pressing reform commitments, Johnstown became a haven to which she often went to rest and recuperate. Sometimes she left her children there when she went on lecture tours, and Harriot Stanton Blatch remembered spending summers in Johnstown with her grandmother and her aunts. She always remained close to her sisters and their husbands, despite their frequent opposition to her reform involvements. They enjoyed her wit and spirit and welcomed her visits, although they usually took care not to discuss woman's rights with her.

Indeed, the independence that her sisters Margaret and Harriet had shown as young girls did not carry over into later life. All her sisters married men close to the family: the husbands of Tryphena, Margaret, and Katherine were all lawyers, as was their father, Daniel Cady. Harriet's husband, Daniel Eaton, was a New York City merchant, but he was the Cady sisters' cousin. The eventual cohesiveness of the Cady family was apparent when, in the 1840s, the Cadys moved to Albany for several years so that Daniel Cady could promote the careers of Margaret's and Katherine's husbands. Among the sisters, Harriet signed the 1848 Seneca Falls woman's rights declaration while on a visit to Cady Stanton, but she withdrew her signature when her husband and father protested.

Only Elizabeth's eldest sister, Tryphena, was involved in public activity. According to Harriot Stanton Blatch she possessed striking executive ability and was a member of the boards of directors of several hospitals and charities in New York City, where she lived. But Blatch found Aunt By, in contrast to her own mother and grandmother, cold, precise, and demanding.

Although Cady Stanton's father never approved of her career as a reformer, he never completely rejected her in later years. For a time he disowned her in his will, but ultimately he revoked the clause. He consistently gave financial aid to his middle daughter and her husband. In 1854 he helped her perfect the final draft of her first speech before the New York State legislature, even though he disapproved of her giving it. His influence over her was strong. Not until after his death in 1859 did Cady Stanton take up a full career as an activist reformer.

Her mother was a different case. Margaret Cady remained intensely proud throughout her life that, as a young woman, she had led the women of her church congregation to triumph over the men in choosing a minister. Ultimately she came to support Cady Stanton's reform activities. In 1867, when Cady Stanton presented woman suffrage petitions to the New York legislature, her mother's name headed one of them. Cady Stanton rarely acknowledged her mother's influence: the harsh maternal personality of her childhood remained too negative a memory. Yet a good deal of Cady Stanton's adult personality was nonetheless an inheritance from Margaret Cady, and her negative reaction to a mother identified with domesticity may indeed have helped her later in demanding freedom within her own role as wife and mother.

The first major crisis in Elizabeth Cady's life occurred in 1826, when she was eleven. In that year her brother, Eleazer, died. Elizabeth was deeply affected by her father's extreme reaction. For months, she remembered, the two of them each evening visited the cemetery near their house. There Daniel Cady would throw himself on the ground above his son's grave, overcome by grief. His consistent response when his daughter tried to comfort him was to bemoan the fact that she was not a boy. Elizabeth responded quickly and directly: she determined to assuage her father's grief by equaling all her brother's achievements, by becoming in effect the male child in the family bereft of sons.

In this first major crisis in her life, she drew on the strength of her developing personality and denied her underlying fears. Her solution presaged her later ability to deal with serious difficulties through positive action rather than through self-destructive brooding. As Cady Stanton realized in later life, her decision to shape her own character had a feminist dimension. "I became a very extraordinary woman," she wrote, "the first of the 'new women,'" using the late nineteenth-century term for liberated women. Youthful experiences of discrimination had only sporadically aroused Elizabeth to a sense of oppression. Although she had realized that her family and her culture preferred boys to girls, she was not yet a committed feminist. But her decision to play the part of a male child symbolized her recognition that independence and self-reliance were the basis of any healthy personality and that girls were not encouraged to develop these traits. Moreover, this decision had important ramifications for her mature feminist ideology. Throughout her career her central purpose would always be to encourage women to be self-reliant, to follow the path, however difficult, she herself had taken.

But she was only eleven. "I thought that the chief thing to be done in order to equal boys was to be learned and courageous," she later explained. "I decided to study Greek and to learn to manage a horse." She put both resolutions into effect immediately, studying Greek with her friend, Parson Hosack, and utilizing the stable of horses which Daniel Cady kept. But her achievements were simply insufficient. Even when she won a prize in Greek at the local academy her father's only reaction was, as always, to express the wish that she had been a boy. And, soon after, when many of her male academy classmates, even those less gifted than she, went off to nearby Union College, she remained behind, disconsolate. In the 1820s no college in the nation admitted women. Yet she could not openly confront her father: so much had the family training in self-control taken hold. She internalized whatever disappointment she felt, and it emerged later in recurrent depression. But ultimately her innate courage overcame her restrictive upbringing, and she took action.

In 1830 Elizabeth Cady entered Troy Female Seminary in Troy, New York. Such boarding schools for girls were common. Usually they catered to the wealthy and concentrated on teaching social skills, like music, French, or manners. But the academy at Troy, known later by the name of its founder, Emma Willard, was more than a mere finishing school. Although Willard paid obeisance to the prevailing ideas about woman's domestic nature, she also stressed self-reliance and offered a teacher training program. At a time when most educators thought girls were neither physically nor intellectually capable of advanced education, Willard tried to give her students an education equal to that of college educated men. Cady Stanton was later critical of the curriculum, judging that the academic subjects were not much more advanced than those taught at the Johnstown academy. She did not like what she thought was an unhealthy attitude about boys and sex. There is a hint that she may have encountered some homosexual activity, not unusual at single-sex boarding schools for adolescents. The commitment to coeducational education, a key part of her later philosophy, stemmed from her negative reaction to Emma Willard's.

Yet predisposed to dislike the seminary, she was pleasantly surprised to find that she enjoyed parts of her experience there. Her classmates were friendly and always ready to follow

her in playing pranks. Dancing, which she loved, was part of
the exercise program. Rigorous training in writing skills, she
later asserted, laid the basis for her literary style. She was
profoundly impressed with Emma Willard herself, whose personality permeated the institution. Willard was distant but
warm, self-controlled, independent, and intelligent. To char-
acterize Willard, Elizabeth Cady used the metaphor for total
female power: the principal was a "queen."

While at Emma Willard's, Elizabeth Cady experienced a
second life crisis. The death of her brother had occasioned a
first turning point; now her religion would become an issue.
In 1831 she attended a series of revivals in Troy conducted by
Charles Grandison Finney. Many early abolitionists, including
Elizabeth's future husband, Henry Stanton, were first drawn to
reform in this same series of revivals conducted throughout
upstate New York. Most listeners responded to Finney's call
for personal reformation and for social reform activity as a way
of demonstrating renewed faith. In contrast, Elizabeth Cady
responded primarily to Finney's strong Calvinism and his use
of vivid imagery stressing hell and damnation. She fell into a
depression so intense that she thought she was going insane.

This time her family came to her aid. Her father, her eldest
sister, Tryphena, and Tryphena's husband, Edward Bayard,
took her on a vacation to Niagara Falls, already a popular
resort. There she recuperated by resting, reading, and discussing theology with Bayard, who questioned the Cady family's
conservatism. To counter Finney's Calvinism, she turned to
several liberal theologians and philosophers. She found the
work of Scotsman George Combe, the foremost philosopher
of phrenology, particularly comforting. Phrenology is com-
monly remembered as a nineteenth-century fad whose practi-
tioners claimed to analyze human personality through the size,
shape, and configurations of the skull, examining the purported "bumps" of the head. But phrenology also had a serious dimension. Combe, for instance, abjured religion to focus
on producing mental health through physical exercise, mental
discipline, and the rational integration of body and mind, and

he had a wide readership among American intellectuals and reformers. In a series of lectures at Troy Seminary in 1831, Almira Phelps, Emma Willard's sister, used the phrenologists' authoritative arguments to urge exercise on the students. The work of Combe and his school would have a profound influence on Elizabeth Cady not only in the resolution of this early crisis but also in the formulation of her mature feminist philosophy. Refreshed by resting and reading, Elizabeth returned from Niagara Falls with her emotions restored. And although she joined her father's church soon after the trip, she had taken her first steps toward religious liberalism.

In the cast of characters at Johnstown as well as at Niagara Falls, Edward Bayard played a central role. Bayard, the son of Senator James A. Bayard of Delaware, had been a classmate of her brother Eleazer at Union College. After Eleazer's death he, along with his brother Henry, had come to study law with Daniel Cady. To a large extent he replaced the deceased son in the family's affections, particularly after he married Tryphena. He was understanding and sensitive. Ten years older than Elizabeth Cady, she thought of him as a second father. To a certain degree he was a rebel; his questioning mind later led him to renounce the law for the practice of homeopathic medicine.

Although homeopaths based their therapeutics on a philosophical system as esoteric as that of regular doctors, they used the standard remedies of bleeding, blistering, and administering vomitives and purgatives only in a limited way, emphasizing instead the body's natural recuperative powers. Homeopathy was the most popular of several alternative medical systems that had appeared in response to the failings of standard therapeutics. By the 1840s there were homeopathic medical colleges and medical societies. Influenced by Bayard, Elizabeth Cady also became a medical skeptic. Throughout her life she advocated natural remedies and homeopathic techniques. Indeed, she taught herself the rudiments of the system and often functioned as an amateur doctor.

Soon after Bayard married Tryphena, they took over the

management of the Cady household because of Margaret Cady's breakdown. The couple had no children—a disappointment which doubled Bayard's affection for the young Elizabeth. He instructed her in fine horsemanship after she decided to learn to ride well, and he persuaded the family to send her to Troy Seminary. When he died in 1889 Elizabeth wrote to her daughter Harriot that she owed much of her childhood happiness to her brother-in-law.

Once Elizabeth Cady graduated from Troy Seminary in 1833, her life took on the aimless quality characteristic of young women of the upper classes between the completion of their schooling and their marriage. She had no thoughts of taking up a career or of becoming a reformer. In fact her first involvement with benevolence left her only indignant. Responding to Protestant Christianity's contemporary crusade to christianize the world through the distribution of tracts and the support of missionaries, Elizabeth headed an association of young women in her family's church to raise money to send an aspiring minister to theological school. Their beneficiary, however, repaid them by preaching a special sermon in the Johnstown church on woman's inferiority. As he began his discourse, his patrons, dressed in their Sunday best and seated in the first row of the church, silently rose and marched from the church in protest, with Elizabeth Cady leading them out.

In these years, Elizabeth spent most of her time riding horseback, helping in her mother's house, reading, and visiting New York friends and relatives. As the Cady daughters grew to maturity, the Cady household was often filled on weekends and holidays with local boys and Union College students. On these occasions, there was probably no dancing, which Elizabeth adored but of which conservative Daniel Cady did not approve. Yet Elizabeth found ways to indulge her love of playfulness. During one party at the Cady house, a suitor from Union College teased her for not being able to stop talking, and she took up his challenge to remain silent while they rode to Schenectady in one of her father's carriages. She easily won the wager by dressing up a feather duster in her clothing and surreptitiously slipping it into the carriage alongside the unsuspecting young man. The story quickly spread among the young people of the area. Elizabeth was applauded for her audacity, while her unfortunate friend became the butt of many jokes at Union College.

Elizabeth Cady later remembered these pleasant years with affection. She always loved fun and frivolity as well as fine clothes, good food, and sleeping late. Yet by 1840 her two older sisters were married, and she was twenty-five and single. Moreover, an unexpected event immeasurably intensified the unresolved elements in her life when Edward Bayard declared his love and pressured her to elope with him. Bayard was unhappy in his childless marriage. He was romantic, intellectual, and fun loving. Tryphena Bayard was down-to-earth and domestic. Elizabeth felt strongly about Bayard, yet realized that elopement would make them pariahs. Sensibly, she rejected his suit. By some feat of self-control she kept knowledge of the incident from the rest of the family and remained on good terms with Bayard and Tryphena for the rest of their lives, even though Bayard apparently refused from then on to be alone with her. For solace she turned to relatives in Peterboro, New York. There, free from conflicts, she met her future husband, a man quite different from Edward Bayard.

Among Elizabeth Cady's many relatives, Gerrit Smith and his family had always been special. Gerrit Smith's father, Peter Smith, who was married to Margaret Livingston Cady's sister, was himself a self-made man. Through astute speculations he had become one of the largest landowners in New York state, and in 1806 had built a baronial mansion and established his own town, Peterboro, in what was still wilderness near Syracuse. In 1819 he turned over the manor and the bulk of of his property to his eldest son, Gerrit, then twenty-two. Only a few years after Elizabeth's birth, Gerrit Smith became the head of the Smith family.

Smith was a commanding person. Energetic and outgoing,

he loved to entertain. Because his home was isolated, he had to import his guests, and interesting people were always at Peterboro: reformers, aristocratic New Yorkers, Southern relatives of Gerrit Smith's wife, and even Oneida Indians, from whom Peter Smith had purchased the land for the estate. Gerrit Smith's wife, Ann Fitzhugh, was intelligent and occasionally dared, in contrast to Margaret Cady and other women Elizabeth knew, to speak her mind openly on controversial issues. Feminist Lucretia Mott later speculated that, in fact, Ann Smith had been responsible for her husband's reform ideas. The Cadys often visited Peterboro, even though it was several days by carriage from Johnstown. At Peterboro dancing, games, and mirth were constant, particularly after the Smiths in the early 1830s renounced the Calvinism which still dominated Elizabeth Cady's home. Playing practical jokes (which Elizabeth loved) was a tradition. The Smith's only child, their daughter Elizabeth, seven years younger than Elizabeth Cady, became a close and lifelong friend.

What was most important at Peterboro by the 1830s was the family's involvement in reform. The Smiths' critical minds searched for the best possible life in service to humanity. By the 1820s, responding to Protestant Christianity's emphasis on benevolence as a means of demonstrating personal regeneration, Smith became a leader of local and state societies concerned with missionaries, tracts, and Sunday schools. However, he was disappointed by the inability of these associations to effect social change, and he slowly moved on to other reform endeavors. By 1830 his primary interest had become temperance; by 1835 he was an abolitionist. In moving from religious benevolence to temperance, a secular reform still centered on personal regeneration, to abolitionism, which focused on social change but still stressed exhortation and regeneration, Smith followed a path common to pre-Civil War reformers.

Elizabeth Cady found visits to Peterboro increasingly exciting. The constant, rousing debates about reform and abolition made social life seem dull and unrewarding elsewhere. Smith's house became a station on the Underground Railroad, and fugitive slaves hid there. Elizabeth never forgot the day that Smith introduced her to a beautiful, eighteen-year-old slave on her way to Canada. She spent several hours telling the young women at Peterboro the story of her life, including her sale at fourteen in the New Orleans slave market for the purpose of prostitution. Perhaps the only important reform not wholeheartedly espoused at Peterboro was woman's rights, although Elizabeth Cady remembered pointing out to the runaway slave her degradation as a woman as well as a black. In spite of Ann Smith's independence, conventional views about woman's role were not absent from Peterboro. In 1836 her daughter, Elizabeth Smith, then at boarding school, wrote to her father in firm agreement with his criticism of women abolitionists who violated the cultural prohibition against women speaking in public.

Many currents in Elizabeth Cady's life came together when, in 1839, on a visit to Peterboro, she met Henry Brewster Stanton, an executive of the American Anti-Slavery Society. Although Stanton had spent some years as a newspaper reporter and minor government official in the Rochester area, he had rarely returned to upstate New York after his own conversion to reform in Charles Finney's revivals but rather had worked as an abolitionist lecturer and organizer in his native New England. His past was romantic. One of the famed 1834 Lane Seminary rebels, he had been a member of Theodore Dwight Weld's original antislavery evangelists in 1836, known as "The Seventy." He had been mobbed on many occasions, and he told tales of subduing crowds by impassioned preaching and of narrowly escaping death.

He was renowned as an antislavery speaker. His eloquence both in personal conversation and in public oratory captivated Elizabeth Cady when she and other Peterboro guests attended meetings he conducted in the area. He was ten years older than Elizabeth—an age differential which had existed in her friendship with Edward Bayard and which was similar to that between her father and mother. A month after they met they were engaged. Stanton's declaration of love was as much a surprise as Edward Bayard's, for she thought Stanton was engaged to another guest at Peterboro.

The announcement brought a storm of protest from Johnstown. The Cadys supported religious benevolence and even temperance, but they regarded the abolitionists as fanatics. Even Edward Bayard opposed abolitionism. For some time Daniel Cady had wanted to prohibit his daughter's visits to Peterboro, but the family connection had made him hesitate. Elizabeth Cady was still vulnerable to her family, and their dire predictions of an uncertain future unloosed once again that anxiety to which she was prey. "Hitherto my apprehensions had all been of death and eternity; now life itself was filled with fears," she wrote. Although Gerrit Smith had a penchant for matchmaking and probably encouraged the romance, even he outlined the difficulties facing the wife of an abolitionist and added to her uncertainty. Once back in Johnstown, she broke the engagement.

However, she soon reversed the decision. Her renewed determination to marry Stanton was partly caprice, partly love, and partly anger at her family. Although Elizabeth was not beautiful, her infectious smile, her welcoming and riveting eyes, her wit, and her boundless energy and sense of fun made her attractive to men. She was plump as a young woman and would become increasingly heavy over the course of her life. But many nineteenth-century Americans found the full figured woman attractive, and Elizabeth did not want for beaux. Had she chosen, she could have married one of the sons of the gentry for whom her parents had prepared her.

In choosing Stanton, Elizabeth turned her back on her Livingston past. Stanton had no money of his own, nor the prospect of inheriting any. Elite society would never accept her as long as he remained an abolitionist. Yet Livingston values had already lost much of their appeal to Elizabeth Cady. In later years she traced her mother's rigidity to her Livingston upbringing and praised her Livingston grandfather only because of his part in the Revolution. She was proud of her colonial and revolutionary ancestry and often referred to herself as a "daughter of the Revolution." But she found all attributes of aristocracy offensive and prided herself on her republicanism, with its overtones of virtue and simplicity and its preference for a natural aristocracy, not one based on inheritance and rank.

Moreover, by 1840, Stanton's abolitionism was a positive attraction. Peterboro and reform had become for Elizabeth Cady much more vital and captivating than the Livingston mansions and their patrician society. One of the few surviving letters from the period of Stanton's courtship is particularly revealing. For in it Stanton pleads his case by detailing his self-reliant past. He, too, was the descendant of colonial and revolutionary forebears, the son of a successful Connecticut merchant and officeholder. But his father had gone bankrupt, and, from the age of thirteen, Stanton had supported himself and had helped two brothers pay for their educations. Like Daniel Cady, Stanton was a self-made man.

Finally, to persuade Elizabeth Cady to marry him, Stanton held out an exceptionally romantic inducement. He had been chosen a delegate to the World Anti-Slavery Convention, to be held in London in June, 1840. The two could combine this event with a wedding tour abroad. To a spirited and intelligent young woman whose life had been confined to upstate New York with occasional visits to New York City, the offer was irresistible. She loved Stanton; the proffered trip was a once in a lifetime opportunity; and the months away might give her family time to accept the situation. Furthermore, when Peter Smith's daughter had earlier married against her family's wishes, Daniel Cady had counseled his relative to accept the situation and had argued that daughters ought to be allowed to marry the men they themselves chose. Elizabeth could hope for an eventually similar response to her own marriage. Above all, Elizabeth Cady had learned upon her brother's death to resolve emotional crisis through action. Now enmeshed again in uncertainty, she followed the same pattern of behavior.

In May 1840, the two were married, hastily and with little

preparation. Elizabeth had made up her mind only a day before the ceremony. Except for her sister Margaret and a few
friends, the Cady family was not there when Stanton came to
Johnstown for the wedding. The next day the newly married
couple traveled to New Jersey to visit Theodore Dwight Weld
and Angelina Grimké Weld, good friends of Stanton and former abolitionists who had married and retired from active
reform involvement. Meeting them might have reassured Elizabeth about the step she had taken.

Angelina Grimké Weld and her sister, Sarah Grimké, who
lived with her, were heroines of the antislavery movement and
feminists in their own right. The daughters of a Charleston,
South Carolina, slaveowner, they came north and became
Quakers and antislavery activists. The public outcry against
them for speaking before audiences which included men had
prompted them to take up the cause of feminism, most notably
in Sarah Grimké's 1838 tract, *Letters on the Equality of the Sexes.*
That same year Weld and Angelina Grimké married and
retired to New Jersey. At first Cady Stanton was chilled by the
austerity of the Welds' ascetic household, which on principle
abjured rich food and decoration. But reminiscences about
Lane Seminary and abolitionist agitation thrilled her and
suffused a glow of heroic idealism about their home that
strengthened her own satisfaction in her marriage. After a
brief stay the Stantons went on to New York City, where they
boarded ship for England.

Elizabeth Cady's marriage was not a total retreat to dependency and domesticity. The brave resolution of an eleven-
year-old to forge a new life of scholarship and self-reliance was
not entirely put aside when romance blossomed. The lessons
she had learned about discrimination against women were not
completely forgotten. In a biographical sketch of Lucy Stone,
Cady Stanton later pointed out that the first action of slaves
freed from bondage was to take a name of their own. Stone,
already a renowned abolitionist and feminist when she married, refused to be submerged in her husband's identity and
kept her own name. Elizabeth Cady also insisted on retaining

her own name, although since she was still young and unknown, she also added her husband's. In addition, by her
request, the minister eliminated from the marital vows the
woman's standard promise to obey her husband. These actions, prophetic of Cady Stanton's later independent stand as
a woman and as a feminist, became general practice among
later nineteenth-century feminists when they married.

I I

Early Marriage and Feminist Rebellion: From London to Seneca Falls

THE STANTONS traveled to London in 1840 for the antislavery cause. But Cady Stanton returned six months later affected not so much by the plight of the slaves as by the situation of women.

The London Anti-Slavery Convention welcomed Henry Stanton as a leading American abolitionist and named him its secretary. Antislavery societies throughout the British Isles invited him to speak. Influential reformers entertained them, and Cady Stanton could hardly believe that she actually met people she "had so long worshipped from afar." The Stantons toured London, journeyed through Ireland and Scotland, and spent time in Paris.

Meetings and discussions with the American women delegates at the convention, however, impressed Cady Stanton more profoundly than the sights or the antislavery issue. The American Anti-Slavery Society, founded in 1833, had divided in 1839 over allowing women to participate in its affairs. New York members, fearing that any association with feminism would undermine abolitionism, wanted women's societies kept separate from the organizations of men. In 1840 they would take leading roles in moving abolitionism boldly into the male world of politics by founding the Liberty party. The Boston and Philadelphia supporters of William Lloyd Garrison, who retained control of the American society, held that both sexes should participate equally in the same societies. In support of their positions, both groups sent delegates to the London convention. But only among the Garrisonians were women to be found.

Before she arrived in London, Cady Stanton's sympathies lay with the New Yorkers. Her husband, active in forming the Liberty party, sided with his New York colleagues, as did Gerrit Smith and the Welds. In addition, James Gillespie Birney, an older abolitionist who was Stanton's close friend and the 1840 Liberty party presidential candidate, was on board their ship. Birney presented a convincing case for the New Yorkers, although he irritated Cady Stanton by criticizing her for what he considered her unwomanly behavior in calling Stanton by his first name in public and in amusing herself by such pranks as persuading the ship captain to hoist her up the mast in a chair. But Cady Stanton did not challenge him. A chess enthusiast, she was grateful to him for playing with her to relieve the tedium of ocean travel. She sensed that Birney, courting a relative of Gerrit Smith, was jealous of Stanton for having his wife along. Furthermore, she felt unsure of her ability to debate the antislavery argument, and was undecided as to how the wife of an abolitionist ought to behave. Henry Stanton was controlled and serious; Cady Stanton worried that she was too "gay and frolicksome."

Her attitude changed when they reached London. The Stantons were lodged in the same boarding house as the women delegates, and they had meals together. Cady Stanton sat next to Lucretia Mott, a renowned Philadelphia Quaker preacher, twenty years her senior, who was the acknowledged leader of the American women representatives. The first night at dinner, despite Birney's frowns and her husband's nudgings under the table, Cady Stanton supported Mott's arguments for woman's equal participation in the antislavery societies. Cady Stanton had always been fascinated by Quaker women, who were allowed to speak-in public and to become ministers and who, like Mott and the Grimké sisters, often took on public roles as reformers. Indeed, Mott was different from the women Cady Stanton knew. She was gentle, serene, and good humored, although she questioned all creeds; she was at peace with herself in defying society's dogmas about women's behavior; and she had the self-confidence to challenge men directly. During the weeks in London, Cady Stanton continually sought Mott out and solicited her views on social and theological issues. Spellbound, she witnessed Mott preach in a London Unitarian church. It was the first time she had heard a woman speak in public before an audience which included men.

At the convention, too, Cady Stanton became Mott's confederate. The question of whether the women should even be accepted as delegates preempted the first days of the meeting. The conservatives were in control. The women were not permitted to speak on their own behalf nor to sit on the convention floor. Instead, they were relegated to a curtained gallery at one end of the hall. Henry Stanton was sufficiently sensitive to his wife's feelings that he, alone among the New Yorkers, spoke in favor of seating the women. Yet, in contrast to William Lloyd Garrison, who was also present, he did not leave his seat on the convention floor to join the women in the gallery. Nor did his advocacy of the women approach the fervor of Wendell Phillips, a patrician Boston Garrisonian whose new wife had been largely responsible for his conversion to antislavery. Wendell and Ann Phillips were also on their wedding trip; the comparison was not lost on Cady Stanton.

The acrimonious debates canvassed all possible arguments for woman's subordination. Cady Stanton found the exchanges "such refined torture as I had never before experienced." The only relief was "the placid comments and smiles of derision that passed around the distinguished circle of women." Barred from speaking at the convention, the women engaged in long debates with the men at their boarding house. After the first such evening, Birney moved to other lodgings. Cady Stanton resolved her anger by a decision to act. She proposed to Lucretia Mott that they hold a woman's rights convention as soon as they returned to the United States, and Mott agreed.

That gathering was not to take place until 1848. Time and other concerns intervened. Mott was committed to antislavery and absorbed in factional Quaker disputes. The impression Cady Stanton made on Mott in London is unclear. Mott's diary makes no mention of the decision to hold a woman's rights convention and only occasionally refers to Cady Stanton, identifying her primarily as the wife of their fellow abolitionist and close friend, Henry Stanton. Later letters indicate that Mott and Stanton became close in London but that theological discussions which the religiously troubled Cady Stanton initiated principally occupied their time.

After the convention the Stantons spent several months traveling. By the fall Cady Stanton was ready to return home. The British minister who escorted them on one of her husband's speaking tours was a rabid antifeminist, even worse than Birney, so she spent a month alone in Dublin rather than deal with his arguments. The rigid class divisions of English society also offended her sense of republican equality, and she was increasingly depressed by the extreme poverty she witnessed.

The return voyage was stormy, and Henry Stanton suffered severely from seasickness. Cady Stanton was delighted to see New York harbor and her waiting relatives once again. Whatever resolves she had made in London to call a woman's rights convention had been eroded by the experiences of the rest of the trip, by her need to come to terms with the inevitable questions of children and domesticity, and perhaps by Henry Stanton's growing belief that the only means to abolitionist success was through practical politics, in the context of which feminism was inflammatory. The couple was also bound for Johnstown and for reconciliation with her family. The prodigal daughter was returning home, and her parents no doubt hoped that Henry Stanton might yet turn out to be the son-in-law they wanted. Her childhood environment, with all its comforts and demands, was no place from which to launch a radical reform.

During the first eight years of her marriage, domesticity dominated Cady Stanton's life. From the beginning, Henry Stanton's career was uncertain, and Cady Stanton's role was necessarily supportive. The antislavery treasury was nearly bankrupt, and Stanton could not count on any continued income from it. Turning to the law, he served his apprenticeship with Daniel Cady while the newly married couple lived with the Cadys. After two years in training, in 1842, Stanton established a practice in Boston, where he was known from his earlier antislavery work and where he anticipated launching a political career and establishing a beachhead for political abolitionism in Garrisonian territory. In Boston, to which Cady Stanton moved in 1843, the insecurities of Stanton's early professional life dictated the continuation of her supportive role.

Many wives of reformers, given the exigencies of their husband's careers, defined themselves in terms of domestic responsibility. Helen Garrison, whose Boston home the Stantons visited, played no part in the abolitionist movement but rather managed a large family on Garrison's small income, entertained a constant stream of visiting reformers, and provided an island of calm in the midst of her husband's frenzied life. When she married, Angelina Grimké Weld had retired from active antislavery involvement. Lucretia Mott had not taken up active reform work until her children were grown. Necessity and example aside, Cady Stanton found the roles of wife and mother deeply fulfilling. Decorating, cleaning, and gardening fascinated her, especially after the Stantons moved into their own home in Boston. Cooking became a passion: "I spent half my time preserving, pickling, and experimenting with new dishes." While still in Johnstown, her first son, Daniel, was born, followed by two more sons, Henry and Gerrit, born during the Boston years. Motherhood added another absorbing interest.

Caring for her children engaged her intellect as well as her emotions. From the birth of her first child, she questioned accepted procedures. The local Johnstown woman she hired as a nurse for Daniel swaddled the infant, tightly wrapping him in strips of cloth which prevented the movement of arms and legs, in the belief that new limbs needed support during the first year of life. She closed the windows to keep out supposed evil substances from the air outside. She counseled Cady Stanton to feed the baby continuously, in the belief that an unfilled stomach caused colic and rickets. She kept on hand an arsenal of herbal concoctions and soothing syrups, many of which contained laudanum, an opium derivative. Despite these attentions, the child cried constantly. Distraught, Cady Stanton "wept, prayed, and philosophized by turns."

She then turned to the available literature on child rearing. Rejecting most treatises as useless, she found validation of both homeopathic medical advice and her common sense in an 1840 work on infant care by Andrew Combe, a Scottish physician and the younger brother of the phrenologist George Combe. Defying her husband, her parents, and her male doctor, she threw off the swaddling clothes, opened the windows to let in fresh air, threw away the medicines, and nursed the baby on a regular schedule during the day and not at night. The results were striking. Although the new schedule monopolized her time as much as the nurse's procedures, the baby stopped crying. And there were other, more personal benefits. She claimed through this experience to have learned "another lesson in self-reliance." Moreover, her involvement in infant care had important ramifications for her later feminist thought, in which she would identify maternity as a key factor in human development.

In neither Johnstown nor Boston did Cady Stanton entirely forego activities outside the home or forget her earlier interest in woman's rights. In both places she found time to study theology, law, and history—particularly as they pertained to women. Before she left Johnstown she took an interest in the Married Women's Property Act, introduced in the New York

State legislature in 1836 and designed to give married women control over their property. The bill had garnered considerable public support, particularly from the wealthy, whose daughters' dowries and inheritances were prey to the debts of bankrupt and improvident sons-in-law. The bill, however, dealt only with property rights; it did not address any of the other legal inequalities of women.

Woman's rights advocates Ernestine Rose and Paulina Wright Davis had already circulated petitions on its behalf. Rose was a follower of radical communitarians Frances Wright and Robert Dale Owen; Davis lectured on woman's physiology and later edited *The Una,* a woman's rights journal. Cady Stanton may have joined them in circulating petitions, and she may have addressed legislative committees on behalf of the property act. But her participation was neither intensive nor extensive. She was still unsure of her own ability in the public realm, unsettled in her views about religion and society, and involved in domesticity.

In 1842 she made her first public speech in Johnstown, not on woman's rights or the property bill for married women, but on the respectable subject of temperance. Her insecurity was evidenced by the fact that she did no more than mention the inflammatory issue of woman's rights in the speech. Nor was she any bolder in private conversation. Defensively, she wrote to Lucretia Mott that she did her best to interject the issue into social discourse. But Cady Stanton did not yet have the courage and self-confidence that speaking out for woman's rights required.

The Stantons' move to Boston in 1843 placed her in the intellectual and reform center of the nation. Margaret Fuller, the transcendentalist intellectual and feminist ideologue whose conversational gatherings with Boston women were renowned, had already left the city. But Cady Stanton seized every opportunity to go to concerts, lectures, plays, and church services. She faithfully attended temperance, peace, prison, and antislavery reform conventions. She met Emerson and Hawthorne and visited Brook Farm, the transcendentalist

commune near Boston—an experience which almost converted her to communitarianism. She remained for the most
part a private person, however. Although she collected signatures on antislavery petitions, she did not become a leader in
any of the reform organizations. On separate occasions she
discussed holding a woman's rights convention with both Lucretia Mott and black abolitionist Frederick Douglass, a recent
escapee from slavery whom she converted to woman's rights
advocacy, but again she did nothing further actually to implement the project.

Yet too public an association with the Garrisonian leaders of
Boston reform might have undermined Henry Stanton's political career. Besides, Cady Stanton still found housekeeping
fulfilling, and religious exploration doubly absorbing in the
national center of religious liberalism. During their first year
in the new city the Stantons boarded with a leading Baptist
minister, who was married to a Livingston relative, and they
participated in constant theological debates at his home. In
1843 Cady Stanton declared that she was thoroughly imbued
with the liberal ideas of Theodore Parker, the well-known
Unitarian theologian, but her "dark Scotch Presbyterian days"
were not far behind her, and she was still in a "hungering,
thirsting condition for truth."

So wary did Boston make her of reform activities that she
continued her woman's rights activity instead in New York, not
in Massachusetts, where, in fact, woman's rights petitions were
not circulated until 1848 and a married woman's property bill
not drafted until 1854. During long visits to her family, both
in Johnstown and in Albany, she continued to circulate petitions on behalf of the Married Women's Property Act, still
pending before the legislature. In Albany, she lobbied on behalf of the bill among the legislators, many of whom she encountered in local society. Again her efforts were modest. But
the experience gave Cady Stanton useful training in politics
and in defending her position before male opponents.

In 1847, after four years in Boston, the Stantons moved to
Seneca Falls, New York. Stanton suffered from chronic lung

congestion in Boston's damp climate; he had failed to win elective office despite several attempts; and he was dissatisfied with the shady ethics of his law partner. Seneca Falls was close to a railroad line to Albany and Johnstown, but it was far enough away from the Cadys' home to keep Stanton and Daniel Cady apart. Cady Stanton's husband and father had come to respect one another, but they conflicted over Stanton's antislavery, liberal politics and his open pursuit of office, which violated Daniel Cady's old school creed that the individual should wait to be drafted. Furthermore, Daniel Cady owned property in Seneca Falls, where Tryphena and Edward Bayard had earlier lived, and, characteristically concerned about his daughter's welfare, he offered the Stantons a house there. Seneca Falls was a growing town, holding out professional possibilities, and it was near the reform centers of Rochester and Buffalo. Down the road in Auburn lived Lucretia Mott's sister, Martha Wright, as well as William Henry Seward, reform governor and antislavery politician. In the nearby town of Waterloo was a large community of reform Quakers.

Yet the situation did not work out as expected. Before the move Cady Stanton worried that Henry would be unhappy in a small town. But the reverse proved to be the case. The years in Johnstown and Boston had been fulfilling for her; the initial months in Seneca Falls were not. Life in her new community revealed years of accumulated grievances, often only dimly perceived at the time. To cope with her discontent and to legitimate her own desire for a broader sphere of action, she began seriously to consider the timeliness of a woman's rights convention. Once again she successfully overcame depression through action; this time her movement toward what, in Emersonian terms, she often called "self-reliance" was almost complete.

More than anything else, Cady Stanton traced her discontent in Seneca Falls to the burden of increased housework. In Johnstown the Stantons had lived with her parents, and in Boston she had always found capable servants. But in provin-

cial Seneca Falls such help seemed unavailable. Her house was
only a block away from the town's most imposing avenue,
along which the wealthy factory owners and merchants lived.
But her street was not paved; it was dusty; and the business
district of town, containing shops and churches and meeting
places, was a good mile or two away.

Domestic tasks that had charmed her in Johnstown and Boston now bored her. Her three children, boys of eight, six, and
three, were difficult to manage, and their activities left the
house in an uproar. From a nearby community of Irish laborers came regular complaints that her boys threw rocks. The
lakes of the area were fertile breeding grounds for mosquitoes,
and respiratory ailments were common. Her children, it
seemed, were constantly sick. For the first time in many years,
Cady Stanton felt directly and personally oppressed as a
woman.

Yet other, deeper reasons lay behind her discontent. In later
years dusty streets and minor illnesses did not bother her, and
she regained her pleasure in domestic tasks. She would then
find substitutes for Boston's cultural life by organizing a town
discussion group, advising neighbors, and bringing friends to
Seneca Falls. But at the moment, all the grievances of her life
in a small town converged with one other mounting problem:
her marriage to Henry Stanton.

Strong-willed and opinionated, Stanton was not easy to live
with. Ten years Cady Stanton's senior, married for the first
time at thirty-five, he was set in his ways. His kindly but nonetheless patronizing control is evident in an 1843 letter in which
he addressed her as "My Dearest Daughter." Two women
abolitionist friends who had traveled with the Stantons for a
brief time in 1840 privately commented on Stanton's over-
bearing treatment of his wife.

Moreover, as a lawyer and politician Stanton simply did not
meet the promise of his early career. Although he devoted
enormous time and energy to volunteer party activism, his
attempts at elective office, except for two terms in the New
York Senate, failed. True, few of the abolitionist militants of

the early 1830s were any more successful as politicians. The later major Free-Soil and Republican politicians, like William Henry Seward, Charles Sumner, or even Abraham Lincoln, were only indirectly connected with militant antislavery. Stanton could hardly escape a past of which he was proud. Henry Ward Beecher analyzed Stanton as a latter-day John Adams, whose adherence to principle made political compromise impossible and who was therefore unpopular among the public.

Yet Beecher was not really correct. Politics more and more became Stanton's ruling passion. His political maneuverings were intricate and intense. He was a founder of the antislavery Liberty party in 1840 and of the Free-Soil party in 1848. In 1849, however, he abruptly changed allegiance to join the so-called barnburner, or antislavery, wing of the New York Democratic party, ignoring the regular Democrats' proslavery stance. Yet the party's antimonopoly and democratic positions attracted him. He was convinced at that point that third parties could not succeed; and he hoped to convert the Democrats to antislavery. In 1849 he finally achieved elective office as a state senator from the Seneca Falls region, supported by a coalition of "barnburners" and free-soil advocates.

Increasingly he left home for long periods on business trips and political assignments. He was absent at the birth of at least two of his children. Whenever possible, he journeyed to Washington to witness the debates in Congress and mingle informally with the politicians. Eventually he became the Washington reporter for the *New York Tribune*. His enthusiasm for politics went beyond the desire to effect social change. He was equally drawn to its masculine nature and the easy camaraderie of men whose careers were based on pleasing others and who usually left their families at home. On the way to Washington, he invariably detoured to Albany to exchange gossip with the state's master politician, Thurlow Weed, on whose newspaper, the *Rochester Telegraph*, he had worked as a reporter in his prereform days. In 1857 Susan B. Anthony noted that Stanton had spent his usual seven months in Washington, pursuing, as she sarcastically put it, "Political Air Castles."

Increasingly Cady Stanton resented his absences and, even more, his freedom to do what he wanted. In 1848 she wrote to a friend of her great love for Henry; in 1858 she poured out her discontent to Anthony. "How rebellious it makes me feel when I see Henry going about where and how he pleases," she wrote. "He can walk at will through the whole wide world or shut himself up alone. As I contrast his freedom with my bondage I feel that, because of the false position of women I have been compelled to hold all my noblest aspirations in abeyance in order to be a wife, a mother, a nurse, a cook, a household drudge."

Stanton's behavior at home also bothered her. The derisive descriptions of American husbands in her writings were clearly modeled after him. The once doting lover had become staid and indifferent, absorbed in his career and his interests outside the home. His pipe and his evening newspapers were irritants that symbolized all the rest. Buried behind his ritual reading, he answered his wife's questions with a vacant stare, while the children were carefully schooled not to disturb "his devotions to his God, his evening paper."

Henry Stanton was not entirely to blame for Cady Stanton's discontent. Both husband and wife liked to live well, but Stanton's income was never large. Daniel Cady gave them their houses in both Boston and Seneca Falls in addition to other financial aid. Nor was Cady Stanton, increasingly strong-willed and opinionated, easy to live with. As early as 1840, on her postwedding visit, the Welds were concerned about Cady Stanton's fashionable ways, and they worried that Henry Stanton was not, in fact, strong enough to guide her in the direction of self-denial and reform. Her son Gerrit contended that his father often went on trips because his mother regularly filled the house with so many visitors that there was hardly room to move. Moreover, after 1848, Cady Stanton's well-known feminism was an obstacle to Stanton's political career, for her reform involvement challenged entrenched cultural conventions about the proper role of women. During Stanton's 1850 campaign for the state senate, a furor was raised because Cady Stanton was wearing the bloomer reform dress, which substituted short skirts and trousers for women's regular long, restrictive dress. Cady Stanton and several other feminists, notably Seneca Falls' editor and Assistant Postmaster Amelia Bloomer, had designed it, and Bloomer's name had quickly been attached to it. Cady Stanton's feminism almost cost Stanton his one elective office.

The Stantons' sexual relationship also was probably a source of frustration. In contrast to many of her contemporaries, Cady Stanton was aware of woman's sexuality, and she agreed with an 1853 phrenological analysis of herself as "able to enjoy the connubial relationship in a high degree." But in her public writings she consistently rated mental and spiritual relationships as more fulfilling than sexual ones and criticized the unregulated sexual drives of men. Her ambivalence about sex probably derived partly from her ambivalence about her own fertility. The Stantons did not practice birth control. Historians now think that knowledge of birth control was widespread in nineteenth-century America. But in her later life Cady Stanton implied that during her childbearing years she was ignorant of such techniques. The many children she bore indicates that she rejected abstinence, although she later stated that at some point after the birth of her third son, Gerrit, in 1845, she began to practice her own eugenic theories about conceiving children only when husband and wife were in optimal condition. The lack of power over her reproductive life increased Cady Stanton's sense of subordination and eventually contributed to the centrality of the birth control message in her feminist theory and activism. In the Seneca Falls years it added to the frustration of an already strained marital relationship.

Despite their difficulties, Cady Stanton never considered divorcing Henry Stanton. She vigorously denied contemporary attacks that her liberal ideas about divorce grew out of her negative experiences with men and insisted that they derived from observations of the experiences of other women, particularly of a childhood friend who discovered shortly after her wedding that her husband had married her only for her dowry. On some level Cady Stanton made adjustments which eased her discontent. She valued Henry Stanton's conversational ability, and she shared his love of gardening. His emotional stability and even temperament were useful in countering her volatility. He was not without a sense of humor, observing at the height of tension over the opposition to the bloomer costume that most men secretly approved it because they could find out if their women friends had fat or thin legs. Finally, Cady Stanton's sense of honor and her commitment to the belief that children conceived in unhappy marriages would suffer severe mental and physical problems was probably too strong to allow her to continue having children with Stanton over a period of seventeen years unless she had been reasonably content.

Cady Stanton expected an enormous amount from marriage: an intense emotional and intellectual relationship, a sense of total union with a soul mate whom she could "reverence and worship as a God." Her writings extolled this kind of union and contrasted it to the usual marriage held together by emotional need, legal entanglement, or the tyranny of husband over wife. Occasionally, however, she described other kinds of imperfect, but workable unions. One such relationship involved two opposite personalities both powerfully attracted to one another and in constant conflict, reflecting her own situation.

Merry and carefree Elizabeth Cady had married strong and sensible Henry Stanton; the romantic idealist and feminist was linked to the pragmatic politician. Yet by and large Henry Stanton did not interfere in her reform activities, no small gesture from a man of his era. He acquiesced to her changes in their marriage ceremony, and did not refuse to be seen with her in bloomer dress, although Susan Anthony claimed that he finally opposed it. As a New York state senator he introduced several woman's rights petitions into the legislature, and he helped her draft the resolutions for the Seneca Falls convention. Although she complained in 1855 that he opposed her advocacy of woman's rights, he rarely interfered with her later career, even when for many months of the year she abandoned her domestic role for nationwide lecture tours and left him at home with responsibility for the family. In 1862 he was the catalyst behind the Woman's Loyal National League, designed to mount a petition campaign to end slavery. At the 1869 organizing meeting of the National Woman Suffrage Association he supported his wife's proposal that membership be limited to women, stating that "he had been drilled for twenty years privately, and he was convinced that women could do it better alone."

Yet there were tensions during all these years. Infuriated, Stanton refused to attend the 1848 woman's rights convention when his wife introduced a resolution for woman suffrage. He was a spokesman for political antislavery; she became a Garrisonian. He supported the Republican stand on Reconstruction, while Cady Stanton mounted a campaign against the antifeminist Fourteenth and Fifteenth Amendments. Returning to his Democratic identification, he supported Horace Greeley for president in 1872, despite his wife's support of Ulysses S. Grant and her bitter controversy over woman's rights with Greeley, a former friend and early supporter of the woman's movement.

Cady Stanton often mused about the unhappy marriages of great men. But it was a self-indulgent half-truth when she implied to her son in 1898 that the function of work in her life had been to "heal her sorrows." Her drive for work, for regular and stimulating occupation, was intense. On some level she discerned that competition with her husband had caused a basic friction in their marriage. Writing after Stanton's death, she recalled how her young son Theodore had praised a speech he heard his father deliver while criticizing one of hers. Rather than accepting the judgment, she traced her son's preference to society's belief in men's superiority. She was perturbed at losing even so minor a competition to Stanton.

Yet the Stantons ultimately worked out some mutually satisfactory arrangement. When the news of Stanton's death reached her while she was visiting her daughter in England in 1887, she felt a deep loss and regretted "every unkind, ungracious word, every act of coldness and neglect." In his autobiography, largely a catalogue of his career, Stanton mentioned his wife only once, referring to her formally, along with Susan B. Anthony, as the leader of the American woman's movement. "We lived together, without more than the usual matrimonial friction, for nearly half a century" was the judgment of her marriage in Cady Stanton's autobiography.

That Cady Stanton became a reformer had little to do with any sense of status discontent, of having lost her social position as the daughter of a weathly judge and the granddaughter of the patrician Livingstons—whether because of her reform activities or because the rise of new commercial elites in economically expanding America had challenged the holders of old wealth for social predominance. Rather than feeling displaced as a daughter of the old elite, she was in sympathy with the new economic order. A committed individualist, she liked laissez faire economics. The egalitarian rhetoric of the Democratic party appealed to her. She chose to make her friends among reformers and individuals outside of the social elite. She liked elegance, but her style of life was informal, not patrician. If anything, her privileged background gave her the motivation and the assurance to reject her past, as many reformers and radicals have often done, such as Gerrit Smith, Wendell Phillips, and the Grimké sisters in her own day, all of whom traced their origins to the elite.

Cady Stanton's decision to become a reformer was an outgrowth of her upbringing, her experiences, her intelligence, her reading, her maternal instincts, and her sensitivity to others. Had she been completely satisfied with her marriage, she might have been content to remain in the background. But once she had made her personal discontent public, the course of events and her considerable ability propelled her into a position of leadership.

In July 1848, after the Stantons had lived in Seneca Falls for nearly a year, Martha Wright, Lucretia Mott's sister, informed Cady Stanton that Mott was due to visit and invited her to spend July 13 with Quaker friends in Waterloo. Present on that occasion were Jane Hunt and Mary McClintock, in addition to Wright, Mott, and Cady Stanton. In the course of conversation, Cady Stanton so eloquently expressed her discontent that she and the others, deeply moved, agreed to convene a woman's rights convention and issue a statement of grievances.

The decision was not as precipitous as it seems at first glance. In April 1848, the New York State legislature had finally passed the Married Women's Property Act. Other states, too, had begun to modify their statutes. Cady Stanton knew that Lucretia Mott regularly visited her sister each year at the time of the regional Quaker meeting. After years of antislavery work, Mott had considerable expertise in the planning of such conventions. The intention of the women at Waterloo was to mobilize reform sentiment only in the immediate Seneca Falls area; they announced the meeting only in the local newspaper and, since it was harvest season, expected a small attendance.

They called the convention for July 19 and 20 and spent a day drawing up an agenda and a declaration of grievances. Developing the latter document occupied most of their time. Again Cady Stanton was the guiding force. She chose the 1776 Declaration of Independence as the model and did most of the actual writing, keeping close to the original phraseology of the eighteenth-century document but substituting the word "male" for the name of "King George." Finding that the Declaration of Independence included eighteen grievances, the women in Waterloo spent most of one day combing law books and other documents to find eighteen injustices of their own. The unexpected difficulty of the task was both frustrating and exhilarating and, drawing on Cady Stanton's particular love of fun, they teased each other about the actuality of their individual oppression. But they felt the gravity of their position as pioneers in a new and radical reform, and laughter relieved their tension.

A half century of feminist thought and writing lay behind their endeavors. They were all familiar with Mary Wollstonecraft's *Vindication of the Rights of Woman* (1792), the first modern feminist treatise; with Sarah Grimké's *Letters on the Equality of the Sexes* (1838); and with Margaret Fuller's *Woman in the Nineteenth Century* (1845). In contrast to these longer works, they intended to present a short and compelling list of grievances on the order of the lawyer's briefs which had been an important part of Cady Stanton's education.

In the end they did not have far to search to discover woman's wrongs. Although married women in some states had secured the right to their own property, they still had no legal right to their earnings or to their children. They could not testify against their husbands in court. Single women could own property, but they paid taxes on it without enjoying the right to vote—the very issue of "taxation without representation" that had triggered the American Revolution. In all occupations women were paid much less than men. The double standard of morality required women to remain virgins until married and then faithful to their husbands, while male indiscretions were condoned. No liberal arts college, with the exception of Oberlin, admitted women. With the exception of writing and schoolteaching the professions were closed to them. Not until 1869 would an Iowa woman be licensed to practice law, and the graduation of Elizabeth Blackwell from Geneva Medical College in nearby Geneva, New York, only a month before the convention was the first episode in a long struggle to secure the regular training and licensing of women in medicine. To Cady Stanton and the others the list of grievances justified the charge of tyranny. In this document they held man to blame for woman's state. "He has endeavored, in every way that he could, to destroy her confidence in her own powers, to lessen her self-respect, and to make her willing to lead a dependent and abject life." In a lengthy series of resolutions, Cady Stanton and the others called for an end to all discrimination based on sex.

Cady Stanton's appropriation of the Declaration of Independence was a brilliant propagandistic stroke. She thereby connected her cause to a powerful American symbol of liberty. She adopted the celebrated felicity of expression of Thomas Jefferson, the author of the original document, who was, in his own time, a proponent of human rights—at least for white men. As did many radicals after her, using the 1776 declaration as the basis of their creeds and manifestoes, she astutely placed her movement within the mainstream of the American tradition and iterated her own loyalty to the revolutionary generation, whom she often identified as "fathers" of the feminists, at least in revolutionary temper. Moreover, her manifesto was in tune with the popular, democratic revolutions against monarchical rule which were sweeping European states in 1848.

Despite the boldness of their action in calling the convention, Cady Stanton and her confederates were seized by insecurity when the convention opened in a local Methodist chapel. On the spot, none of them had sufficient self-possession to chair the meeting. They pressed James Mott, Lucretia Mott's husband, into service, even though the women had previously agreed that men should not take part in the event. But their audience of 300 was much larger than they had expected, and it included forty men. The Waterloo Quakers were there in full force, as were representatives from the Rochester reform community, including black abolitionist Frederick Douglass. In Seneca Falls the meeting was a major event, and it attracted many townspeople, including aggrieved women factory workers, committed reformers, and the curious.

The first day of the convention was devoted to speeches by Mott, McClintock, and Cady Stanton, among others. When Cady Stanton took the podium, the prospect was so threatening, she later recalled, that she felt like "suddenly abandoning all her principles and running away." Amelia Bloomer, who along with her husband managed the Seneca Falls post office, contended that Cady Stanton spoke so softly it was impossible to hear her. Yet by the second day, which was devoted to reading the Declaration of Sentiments and voting on its resolutions, Cady Stanton was sufficiently bold to electrify the meeting with a new and controversial resolution. She proposed that the Declaration of Sentiments demand suffrage for women. All other resolutions passed unanimously. But only a bare majority voted in favor of suffrage and only after an eloquent speech by Frederick Douglass.

The Quakers at the convention opposed the demand for suffrage because, as pacifists, they abjured any participation in a polity that condoned war as national policy. But there was much more to the opposition than that. Henry Stanton, the reformer, helped his wife draft the resolutions for the convention. But Stanton, the politician, refused to attend when his wife decided to introduce the suffrage resolution. Even Lucretia Mott contended that the demand would make them appear ridiculous.

The exclusive right to vote, Stanton and Mott knew, was central to male political hegemony. Early in the century state legislatures had disenfranchised women in the states where colonial voting rights were still theirs, just as they had disenfranchised free blacks in the 1820s and 1830s when they eliminated property qualifications for voting and instituted universal male suffrage. The democratization of American politics coincided with an increasing conservatism with regard to the position of women and an increasing tendency to define their proper role as domestic. Democracy and the free enterprise economy created a volatile social order in which neither status nor income was entirely secure. In compensation, the society reinforced traditional definitions of separate masculine and feminine spheres of behavior, particularly after the woman's rights movement challenged it. Republican ideology, which was a legacy of the Revolution, and the religious revivals of the 1820s and 1830s, in which most converts were women, both centered on purifying the nation; and both regarded woman's natural virtue and influence in the home as primary agents of national regeneration. The rough worlds of business and politics were for men; women provided a secure haven in the home and through it attempted to institute moral reformation.

The average politician, patterning himself after Andrew Jackson, strove to be forceful and aggressive. Martin Van Buren was ridiculed for his elegant manners: the age's worst epithet, "man-milliner," with its pejorative reference to effete male hatmakers, dogged him throughout his career. William Henry Harrison underscored his identity by adopting as his symbols the coonskin cap and the whiskey barrel—potent symbols of masculinity. The political world was masculine, its competitiveness symbolized by party battles and ritualized by tempestuous elections, in which heavy drinking and fist fights were the order of the day at the saloons and barber shops where many polls were set up. When Lucretia Mott described the demand for suffrage as "ridiculous," she meant that the culture would view the entry of women into the political world as so outlandish as to seem comical.

To Cady Stanton, the daughter of a statesman and the wife of a politician, the political world was neither strange nor impregnable. For years her husband had argued that politics was the key to abolitionist success; it was a primary source of power in the democratic polity. It was no less the key to feminist success, Cady Stanton came to understand, and the vote was the first step. Nor was suffrage potentially as culturally explosive as other radical ideas, like divorce reform or birth control, which were becoming crucial to Cady Stanton's emerging ideology, and which she avoided at Seneca Falls. In her personal experience and her own ideology, the demand for suffrage was pragmatic, not radical.

Furthermore, for years Cady Stanton had resented her husband's preoccupation with politics. It is not surprising that she chose the issue of woman's access to politics as her first significant act of feminist rebellion. As early as the spring before the convention she had approached New York legislator Ansel

Bascom, a former classmate at Johnstown Academy and a Seneca Falls neighbor, to suggest that he introduce a woman suffrage bill before the legislature. In addition, in August 1848, just a few weeks after the Seneca Falls convention, political abolitionists, among whom Henry Stanton was prominent, were to meet to form a new Free-Soil party that would appeal as much to the economic ambitions of Northerners as to their antislavery sentiment. Henry Stanton stormed out of Seneca Falls; any connection with the controversial issue of woman suffrage might seriously damage the future of the new party, as well as his own career within it.

In advocating a position that varied from that of other feminists, Cady Stanton established her mature reform style. Within the context of reform politics and prevailing social attitudes, the emphasis on enfranchisement was radical. It was calculated to shock woman's rights advocates into a stand that would directly confront social prejudices and prove that they lacked neither courage nor commitment. As was her wont, Cady Stanton gave a number of explanations for introducing the suffrage resolutions in the 1848 convention. First, she contended that it was based on the advice of Daniel O'Connell, leader of the Irish independence movement. When she asked him at a dinner party in Dublin in 1840 whether he really expected to achieve separation from England, he replied that in order to achieve any advance, he always made extreme demands. Frederick Douglass, who had told her that the vote was the major means to achieve equality for blacks, was another source of the suffrage resolution. The abolitionists had not yet put forward such a radical demand; Cady Stanton decided that the feminists would.

Above all, her model was William Lloyd Garrison. She had criticized his militant style during the London Anti-Slavery Convention and in 1841 declared her support for her husband's advocacy of political action. But even then she was wavering, writing of her partial conversion to Garrison's ideas. His early support of woman's rights always impressed her. Nor did she forget his willingness to choose principle over politics;

his role in the abolitionist movement as prophet and moralist deeply appealed to her. Garrisonian strategy recognized that the number of dedicated abolitionists was too small ever to be more than a pressure group and that the very nature of politics inevitably compromised their goals. The key to antislavery success lay therefore in changing public opinion and not in party action.

To Cady Stanton the parallels with woman's rights were strong. Despite her husband's involvement in the antislavery political parties and his emergence as one of Garrison's major antagonists, by 1852 she judged the Liberty party and the Free-Soil party to be failures, not successes. Neither had achieved significant electoral victories, and the Free-Soilers, in her view, had compromised too many antislavery principles in their drive for power. "The history of the antislavery agitation," she wrote, "is on this point a lesson to thinking minds." The political abolitionists had failed because they had "trusted to numbers to build up a cause, rather than to principles, to the truth and right." She further underscored her Garrisonian strategy of political action when she wrote: "I would give more for the agitation of any question on sound principles, thus enlightening and convincing the public mind, than for all the laws that could be written or passed in a century. By the foolishness of preaching, must all moral revolutions be achieved."

Throughout her career Cady Stanton was pulled toward the opposite poles of politics and morality and of partisan maneuver and direct confrontation. That she usually chose confrontation and a high moral stance over indirect political methods had much to do with her emotional makeup. Politics was not really congenial to her. Independent by nature, with a childlike love of surprises, impatient of partial solutions and unable to tolerate delay, the political mode of moderation, compromise, and slow progress did not fit her. Rather she preferred to shock her colleagues, to stir them out of complacency, to arouse their passions through introducing issues they had not considered. Furthermore, emotionally volatile, powerful in personality, and liking extravagant praise, the platform and the lecture hall, not the assembly chamber, appealed to her. She loved the theater and often suggested that acting was an exciting career for women. She became a brilliant interpreter of feminist ethics as a writer and orator and not as a political strategist. She attributed her successful effort for suffrage at Seneca Falls to arguments delivered from the public podium and not in private conversation.

Had the Seneca Falls convention not occurred, the woman's rights movement would nonetheless have shortly come into being. Groups in Ohio and Massachusetts were contemplating action, and the Seneca Falls declaration called for similar meetings throughout the nation. Indeed, Boston reform women, former associates of Cady Stanton, in 1850 organized the first woman's rights convention purposefully designed to be national in scope in the reform center of Worcester, Massachusetts. Nonetheless the legend of the primacy of Seneca Falls was quickly established. No other meeting produced such a powerful document as its Declaration of Sentiments, and the immediate and nationwide reaction of the press quickly gained it public notoriety. The telegraph and the newly formed Associated Press quickly disseminated the news of the meeting. Until then, newspapers had paid little attention to woman's rights activities; all those present at Seneca Falls were amazed at the ferocity of the medium's response.

Somewhere they had touched a raw nerve. Whether out of fear or disdain, whether because all editors were men and most newspapers were quasi-official organs for political parties, the press was vituperative in denouncing the meeting. They advanced charges that would become characteristic of the opposition to feminism throughout the century: the leaders were frustrated old maids; the demands were unnecessary because most American women, pampered by husbands and fathers, were satisfied with their lots; and abandonment of the domestic sphere threatened marriage, the family, and the entire social order.

Cady Stanton later asserted that, had she realized the furor the convention would rouse, she would never have called it.

Indeed, she opposed having a woman chair a convention held two weeks later in Rochester to continue the discussions. Of the 100 men and women who signed the declaration, many retracted their signatures under pressure from relatives. When Daniel Cady heard about the meeting, he hurried to Seneca Falls, along with his son-in-law, Daniel Eaton, whose wife Harriet had been visiting Cady Stanton and had signed the declaration. Under pressure from her father and her husband, Harriet retracted her signature and returned home. But despite the entreaties of her father, Cady Stanton refused to withdraw her name. She would not recant. In calling the Seneca Falls convention, in writing the declaration, in holding firm for suffrage, she had taken her stand. In the process, she had found herself.

III

Motherhood, Reform, and Feminism: The Seneca Falls Years
1848–1862

THE SENECA FALLS convention marked the beginning of Cady Stanton's mature commitment to feminism. It also signaled the lifting of the first serious depression to trouble her since her marriage. "It cleared her mind," wrote her daughter, Margaret. In later years she was renowned for the serenity and self-control that she had earlier admired in Emma Willard and Lucretia Mott, for an optimism and self-confidence which were the results of an act of will. She had made herself into the image of what she wanted to be. She wrote that she never encouraged sad moods. Rather, physical labor or concentration on practical subjects brought on the feeling that "all is well, grand, glorious, triumphant." When a black mood came over her, she often cleaned the house from cellar to attic.

Even childhood responses to hurt or frustration now became strengths. Her tendency to sleep when angry or depressed became an ability to sleep at will. Many afternoons she napped when watching her children in their playroom, in the midst of their noise, so that she could stay up late writing. She could sleep in train stations, in jolting wagons, in the backstage areas of theaters. She considered this ability to be the secret behind her enormous energy.

Doubts about religion ceased to plague her. The family attended the local Episcopal church, not exactly by her choice, but because her sons had looked into the building on a Sunday walk and had found the minister's "nightgown" fascinating. Subsequently she decided she liked the music, the ceremony, and the minister's preaching at the Episcopal church. Henry Stanton, however, often attended the Presbyterian church. When Stanton came home from one of his trips with renewed interest in the preaching of Charles Grandison Finney, whom he had heard in New York City, Cady Stanton with apparent ease dismissed revival religion as an enthusiasm. By this point her conversion from traditional Christianity to religious liberalism was complete. Although denunciations of the Protestant ministry for antifeminist manipulation of women would be a staple of her rhetoric, she had emancipated herself from the religious uncertainties that had earlier entangled her. Prophetically, she wrote that she could now defer theological speculations to old age.

Stanton's absences, the pressures her Johnstown family exerted on her to stay at home, her own concern over entrusting to others the raising of her children were serious obstacles to the active reform career that her actions at Seneca Falls implied. For fulfillment, she looked in other directions. She had always loved parties and play, gaiety and society. Her skills in conversing and listening, her energy and enthusiasm drew the people of Seneca Falls to her. Her door was always open, cakes and juice on the table. After the birth of each of her four Seneca Falls children, she unfurled a flag atop her flagpole—red for a boy, white for a girl—to let her friends know they could visit. The leaders of Seneca Falls' high society often shunned her because of her feminist involvements, but she was a catalyst for the rest of the community. Assistant Postmaster Amelia Bloomer once forwarded a letter to her at Johnstown and noted on the envelope, "People have nothing to talk about while you are gone."

Cady Stanton also dealt with Seneca Falls as a reform stage in miniature. Committed to health reform, she set up a small gymnasium in her barn for neighborhood children. She convinced town officials to provide special classes for girls excluded from town supported calisthenics. Borrowing from the example of Margaret Fuller's famed Boston conversations, she organized evening discussion groups in which the participants met at each member's home in turn, gave papers, selected a leader, and discussed a chosen topic. In contrast to Fuller's discussion groups, however, men were included, the topic did not always concern women, and no single person dominated, although Cady Stanton complained on at least one occasion that men seized control of the discussion. Reflecting her own predilections, the evenings often ended with music and dancing.

She also served as a counselor to troubled individuals. The nearby Irish families brought their problems, including their medical complaints, to her. Equipped with herbs and a homeopathic manual, she became adept at doctoring and even delivered babies. Many people consulted her for financial, legal, and personal advice, particularly women with marital problems. The stories she heard in these sessions fueled her growing interest in liberal divorce laws.

Raising her children also became an opportunity for experimentation in reform. Cady Stanton wrote only scattered articles about child rearing. But it was a central concern that both reflected and shaped her mature feminist ideology. In reaction to her own strict upbringing and in accord with contemporary trends towards permissiveness, Cady Stanton refused to discipline her children. Regarding them as rational beings with rights of their own, she dealt with their waywardness through reasoned discussion. Abhorring the fear of God and of adult authority which was central to traditional methods of education in self-control, she taught the young Stantons to rely on their own judgment. Self-control, she believed, grew out of self-knowledge and not out of anxiety and guilt.

Above all, she tried to encourage in her children independence and self-reliance, qualities which were a central theme in her own biography, in her feminism, and in much of the popular writing of the day. The children's piano teacher remembered how Cady Stanton refused to order a recalcitrant Theodore to practice the piano but pointed out to him instead the benefits of doing so; Cady Stanton even refused to awaken her children early in the morning because she believed that they should get up by their own motivation. Drawing on her childlike love of fun, she also regularly joined her children in their games. She encouraged her daughters as well as her sons physically and mentally to exert themselves in preparation for lives of achievement. She did not transfer her resentment against Henry to them: Margaret remembered him during the Seneca Falls years primarily as a generous father who, although often away, brought wonderful presents to them.

Cady Stanton handled her roles as wife, mother, writer, reformer, social leader, and counselor with skill and success. Even in the early years, her achievements gave her a sense of triumph. Symbolically, she put her strength to the test in 1852 when, pregnant with her fifth child, she decided to challenge the standard belief that childbirth was the supreme example of a woman's weak physiology by proving it was a natural experience. During the pregnancy she regularly exercised, and she took a three mile walk the night before the birth. She felt indomitable when, after undergoing labor with only her housekeeper and a nurse present and delivering the baby herself, she resumed her normal routine immediately, even though everyone she knew predicted that the regimen would kill her. That the child was a girl, her first daughter, Margaret, gave her special pleasure. At the time of birth Henry Stanton was away; perhaps that was the way, finally, she wanted it.

But there were substantial problems. Raising seven children almost single-handedly was not easy, especially given her permissive techniques. In 1852 Cady Stanton finally found an able housekeeper who relieved her of some of the burden and who stayed with the family until the children were grown. But she still complained of her own duties. Both her son Gerrit and her daughter Harriot in later memoirs expressed hostility because of her involvements outside the family. Her rambunctious elder boys were a constant irritant; permissiveness only increased their rebelliousness. Eventually she sent them to the New Jersey boarding school that Theodore Weld and Angelina Grimké Weld had established.

Occasionally she felt the loneliness of isolation from reform centers and from her friends, particularly since Lucretia Mott's sister, Martha Wright, who lived nearby, traveled great distances to attend woman's rights conventions, despite her comparable responsibilities as the mother of six small children. Even in 1852, the year of her first daughter's birth, of the hiring of an expert housekeeper, and of her election to the presidency of the state woman's temperance society, Cady Stanton wrote Elizabeth Smith Miller that she had decided against naming her daughter after any of her friends because of the fleeting nature of friendship. The comment was unintentionally ironic. The previous year she had met Susan Anthony and had begun a celebrated friendship that would span both their lifetimes and in itself encapsulate the history of the nineteenth-century woman's movement. In the 1850s the friendship would help her to endure, but not indefinitely to accept, the frustrations of marriage and of life in a provincial mill town.

During the Seneca Falls years, Cady Stanton attempted to remain active in woman's rights organizations. She wrote articles, spoke at nearby churches and lyceums, and circulated woman's rights and suffrage petitions. She lent her name to convention announcements. She opened her home to reformers on their way to engagements in the reform belt from Ohio and western Pennsylvania through upstate New York to western Massachusetts and Boston. Among her guests were Lucy Stone and Antoinette Brown, who were graduates of Oberlin College. Although not present at the 1848 convention, they were both important antislavery and woman's rights lecturers. Stone would become a major woman's rights leader, Brown the nation's first ordained woman minister. Their visits kept Cady Stanton involved in the larger movement.

Yet of the many woman's rights conventions after 1848, Cady Stanton attended only those in nearby Rochester or in Albany near her parents' Johnstown home. She was simply too committed to her children to leave them with a nurse in Seneca Falls. An incident which occurred in Albany and which she recounted numerous times indicates her underlying guilt at the prospect of leaving her children in the hands of others while she pursued a public career. The episode also reveals her scarcely submerged anger at the cultural demand that mothers bear total responsibility for their children. Following a speech she delivered, several women in the audience challenged her for having deserted her children. To her relief she was able to retort that they were with a nurse in her nearby hotel room. Using a characteristic debate technique, she turned the rebuke against her challengers and asked them what they had done with their own children while listening to her. In contrast to politicians or women of fashion, she continued, with veiled allusion to her husband's behavior, she never left her children to go to "Saratoga, Washington, Newport, or Europe."

To the conventions that Cady Stanton did not attend, she wrote public letters designed to rouse the delegates to action. For example, to the 1851 national convention in Ohio she outlined a stirring program, including petition campaigns in every state, demonstrations at every election, concerted efforts to enter the professions, and refusal to pay taxes as long as women were denied governmental representation—the last in imitation of revolutionary precedent. However, her absences necessarily restricted her influence on policy.

Yet the reform situation was complex. The enthusiasm which the 1848 convention had engendered withered in the face of opposition. But it did not die. Rather it seemed to energize many women into asserting themselves in other, more socially acceptable reforms, primarily temperance. Amelia Bloomer described how in Seneca Falls women who found woman's rights too radical organized a temperance society shortly after the convention because they realized for the first time "that there was something wrong in the laws under which they lived." Moreover, in these years New York State was alive with reform agitation. William Lloyd Garrison held a series of inflammatory antislavery rallies. To test the 1850 fugitive slave law, abolitionists in upstate New York made several dramatic rescues of escaped slaves who had been arrested and introduced several emotionally laden test cases in the courts. The presidential election campaigns of 1848 and 1852 were especially volatile, with constant speakers and rallies throughout the state.

"The whole people," wrote Cady Stanton, "seemed to be on the watch towers of politics and philanthropy." Men had been involved in temperance activity since the 1820s. Now women, whose major reform involvement had previously been religious benevolence, joined the crusade, especially since the legislature repealed an 1846 law strictly licensing liquor outlets. "The burning indignation of women, who had witnessed the protracted outrages on helpless wives and children in the drunkard's home," according to Cady Stanton, prompted many to take the public platform, to smash bottles and mirrors in saloons and attack liquor dealers, and to form temperance organizations.

Among reform causes, temperance in particular had a feminist dimension. Woman's temperance societies focused on reducing the spread of alcoholism throughout the nation, but they also assumed that excessive drinking was a male problem with serious consequences for women. The underlying thrust of their appeal was not so much to reform society as to reform men. In principle, Cady Stanton supported temperance. She had been raised in a temperance family and had lectured for temperance in the 1840s. She often repeated the story of a friend whose three sons had died from alcoholism. However, in contrast to committed temperance advocates, Cady Stanton regarded alcoholism as a symptom of the despotism of men over women and not as its source. Ending excessive drinking would not end male tyranny; for that fundamental changes in laws and attitudes concerning women were needed.

However, even in Seneca Falls, little enthusiasm could be roused for a woman's rights society, and Cady Stanton did not attempt to organize one. When in 1852 she sponsored a special lecture on woman's physiology, fewer than fifty of the town's 3,000 women attended. Margaret Stanton remembered at least once running away from a crowd of children jeering, "Your mother believes in woman's rights!" Yet, as in other towns throughout the North, the Seneca Falls Woman's Temperance Society flourished. Drawing on the strategy of feminists elsewhere who faced a similar situation, Cady Stanton moved slowly toward an alliance with temperance forces with the hope of gaining support for feminism. Now for a brief time, perhaps influenced by her husband's political maneuverings, Cady Stanton experimented with the most political scheme of her career. In the end, she failed, for she had not yet realized the conservatism of women—even those involved in social reform.

In the summer of 1849 she began to write for Amelia Bloomer's new woman's temperance journal, *The Lily*. At this point, woman's magazines rarely ventured beyond the standard fare of piety, domestic advice, and fashion information. *The Lily* was important because of its social reform emphasis and its wide readership among temperance women. In addition, Cady Stanton eventually convinced Bloomer, a moderate, to support woman's rights. At first Cady Stanton wrote on child care, education, and temperance. To conceal authorship by a notorious feminist, she used the pseudonym "Sunflower." In January 1850, her first woman's rights article appeared, and subsequently she began to use her own name.

Dress reform also drew Cady Stanton's attention for it seemed practical and potentially popular, and, like temperance, offered a way of awakening women to an understanding of their oppression. For some time conservative doctors and health reformers had railed against women's fashions. With innumerable petticoats, skirts trailing in the mud, and tightly laced waists, women's clothes damaged their bodies. At the spas and sanitariums established by medical rebels who purveyed a regimen of healthy food, exercise, baths, and massages, loose fitting garb was worn. *The Lily* had publicized the short dress designed by popular actress Frances Kemble, and reader response had seemed favorable. On her wedding trip Cady Stanton had extemporized a similar costume when she and Stanton went hiking in Scotland. In 1850, Gerrit Smith's daughter, Elizabeth Smith Miller, now married, came to visit. A moderate feminist, she wore a costume of baggy trousers and a short dress, of her own design. Her appearance seemed final proof that there existed, as Cady Stanton put it, "a serious demand for some decided steps, in the direction of a rational costume for women." Bloomer, Cady Stanton, and most woman's rights advocates soon adopted Miller's garb. Publicized in *The Lily*, the dress acquired the popular name of "bloomer" after its chief publicist rather than its creator.

No one who adopted the bloomer costume expected quite the furor it engendered. Miller had devised it because of the difficulty of doing housework, caring for children, and walking on unpaved roads in regular dress. Cady Stanton immediately realized its practical value and found it a personal boon. For several years she remained optimistic that women would adopt the new style. In 1853 she encouraged Elizabeth Smith Miller, disheartened, to "stand firm a little longer." It was inconceivable that they should not soon be "a respectable and respected majority." Even then, however, Cady Stanton was wavering in her own resolve. Lucretia Mott had feared that the demand for the ballot would make woman's rights advocates appear ridiculous. As it turned out, the bloomer costume had exactly that effect. The opposition was more vitriolic than anything feminists had yet experienced. Newspapers unfairly accused the bloomers-wearing women of advocating not only woman's rights but also an end to marriage and the family. Graphic artists caricatured them as outrageously masculine or as alarmingly ugly old maids. Even small boys taunted women who wore bloomers on public streets. All Cady Stanton's Johnstown relatives pressured her to give it up, and even her sons at school in New Jersey criticized her for wearing it.

Instead of petitioning male legislators to grant changes, as they had done in the past, women here had seized the initiative and themselves had instituted a highly visible change. Furthermore, the new costume included trousers, which was its final undoing. The derision voiced by antifeminists often included fantasies of Amazonian women seizing male prerogatives and focused on their wearing trousers, the symbol of male authority, as the final indignity. By the end of 1853, Cady Stanton herself gave up wearing bloomers in public because she could no longer stand the criticism. She was the first feminist leader to do so.

Yet Cady Stanton never really considered the bloomer costume attractive. She thought the trousers and short dress were ungainly and lacked the graceful lines of regular dress. Cady Stanton was vain about her appearance, and she loved fine clothes. Too little was gained, she found, by trumpeting feminism in her attire and alienating strangers before she could get on with more important issues. Stylish dress disarmed the opposition and cloaked her radical views with respectability. She wore comfortable clothes at home, but after 1853 she never again wore the reform dress in public.

Concurrently with the bloomer campaign, Cady Stanton continued her work with temperance. To what extent, however, she could broaden her feminist involvement remained problematic as long as she was bound to Seneca Falls and her family. Then in 1851 she met Susan B. Anthony, who had come to Seneca Falls for one of Garrison's rallies. In subsequent years the two women formed a friendship which was crucial to Cady Stanton's ability to operate in a broader sphere.

In 1851 Anthony was a resident of Rochester. Several years before she had given up her fifteen-year career as a schoolteacher to help out on her father's farm and to work for temperance. Although she was sympathetic to woman's rights, she had not attended the Seneca Falls convention. Amelia Bloomer, who knew Anthony through temperance circles, introduced her to Cady Stanton in passing on a street corner.

Preoccupied with thoughts of the mischief her boys, at home alone, might get into and with plans for entertaining Garrison and several others who were staying with her, at first Cady Stanton paid little attention to the younger, unknown Anthony.

Over the next year the relationship deepened. During the summer of 1851 they spent time together when Anthony, along with Lucy Stone and other reformers, met for several days at Cady Stanton's home to discuss establishing a progressive college in the area—an effort which proved abortive. By the spring of 1852 Anthony engineered Cady Stanton's election as president of the New York State Woman's Temperance Society. By 1853 Anthony had become so close to the Stanton family that she was given charge of the infant Margaret's weaning.

In the bond between these two women, as in most powerful human relationships, there was an inexplicable chemistry. Such strong friendships between women were common in nineteenth-century America, an outgrowth of the extreme separation of sex roles and of the distinct male and female worlds of education, entertainment, and occupation. Moreover, in an age unaware of the existence of lesbianism, there was no public suspicion of a possible sexual component to inhibit close friendships among women. Woman's rights advocates were often attacked as "unsexed" and "Amazons," but the poetry of Sappho had high sales in Victorian America. There is no evidence that Anthony's and Cady Stanton's friendship was ever more than mental and emotional, and the closeness they achieved was not atypical of friendships among women in their age. In contrast to most major woman's rights activists, Anthony was unmarried, but she was attracted to children and family life. She was six years younger than Cady Stanton, who in the beginning played the satisfying role of counselor to a friend who felt conflicts similar to those which had troubled her in earlier years. Throughout their relationship Cady Stanton called Anthony "Susan," but she was always "Mrs. Stanton" to her friend.

The core of the friendship was a blend of opposites; and in this case, the opposite characteristics were complementary. Cady Stanton was vivacious, fun loving, and a brilliant conversationalist with a biting sense of humor. Anthony was stern, controlled, introspective, and insecure about her writing and speaking abilities. She was dazzled by Cady Stanton's oratory and writing, by her radical style, and by her apparent fearlessness of consequences when she decided to take up a cause. Cady Stanton, for her part, shrank from administrative work: organizing committees, arranging for halls, soliciting funds, even doing research. She liked theory and ideas; she disliked facts. Anthony, on the other hand, was a natural administrator and an indefatigable researcher. Theory bored her; she responded best to details. Anthony came to Cady Stanton's home laden with books and articles to fill in the details of the speeches and resolutions which Cady Stanton created. Anthony often took over the housework and the children. The two planned strategy together, and Anthony carried it out. As Cady Stanton described their early partnership, "I forged the thunderbolts and she fired them."

Moreover, personal confrontation was painful to Cady Stanton. She often found it difficult to disagree with close friends in private conversation. So strong was her desire to please—a legacy of her upbringing—that once she had extended an invitation to her home, she was unable to withdraw her hospitality. Upon occasion her home became so crowded with reformers and other visitors that, rather than directly asking guests to leave, she packed up her family and escaped to Johnstown. Her mature reform style reflected her dislike of personal controversy. At Seneca Falls she adopted the approach of making her position so public that no one could be unclear about her stance and of utilizing her substantial ability at formal debate to avoid informal confrontation. The friendship with Anthony was an additional aid, for, as all who knew them agreed, when they took a position on any issue, "their faith in their united judgment was immovable."

In the early years, Anthony was also close to Lucy Stone and

Antoinette Brown, both of whom faithfully attended temperance and woman's rights conventions and who, like Anthony,
seemed bent on permanent spinsterhood. But these friendships cooled when in the mid-1850s Stone and Brown married
Henry Blackwell and Samuel Blackwell, brothers of Elizabeth
Blackwell, America's first woman physician. Subsequently they
both had children, retired from reform, and became increasingly conservative. Moreover, both Stone and Brown took
umbrage at Anthony's frequent criticism of their marriages
and pregnancies, but Cady Stanton had the ability to laugh at
her friend's complaints.

The relationship between Anthony and Cady Stanton was
not without tension. Anthony was often angry with her friend
for having so many children, for disliking conventions, and for
paying so little heed to details. From the late 1860s on they
often disagreed on ideology and strategy and several times
came close to public confrontation. Yet that the relationship
appear flawless was important to both of them, particularly to
Anthony, who remained Cady Stanton's idolater while many
other movement leaders criticized her. Anthony always insisted that Cady Stanton be chosen president of woman's
organizations they led and remained faithful to feminist hagi-
ography which lauded Cady Stanton as the founder of the
movement. Among feminists their friendship took on epic pro-
portions. It was a striking example of the spiritual relationship
exalted by nineteenth-century romantics. It gave the lie to the
common assumption that women, presumably petty by nature
and in competition for men, could not be friends with one
another. It was forged in adversity, as well. Together Anthony
and Cady Stanton fought the battles of the 1850s and 1860s
for such radical issues as woman suffrage, divorce, and the
rights of working women—and their allies were few.

The friendship was also crucial to Cady Stanton's reform
participation. She often reflected that without Anthony's support she might have abandoned reform for domesticity. "With
the cares of a large family," she wrote, "I might, in time, like
too many women, have become wholly absorbed in a narrow

family selfishness." On the other hand, Anthony, unattached, was mobile. Her initial involvement was with the temperance reform which Cady Stanton wanted to radicalize. In contrast to many in the woman's movement, she was sympathetic to Cady Stanton's radical ideas. Through Anthony, Cady Stanton could pursue the broader goals denied her by confinement to Seneca Falls. "Night after night by an old fashioned fireplace we plotted and planned the coming agitation," wrote Cady Stanton. "Speedily the State was aflame with disturbances in temperance and teachers' conventions, and the press heralded the news far and near that women delegates had suddenly appeared demanding admission in men's conventions."

In January 1852, the New York Men's State Temperance Society invited women's societies to send delegates to their annual meeting in Albany. Susan Anthony was among them. Once there, she discovered that the men would not allow the women to take part in the proceedings. Their apparent design was to gain control over the women's societies, not to admit them as equal partners. Anthony was outraged. Drawing on her natural boldness and her Quaker heritage, she had the temerity to object. But once she rose to speak, she was ruled out of order. When she attempted to proceed, the male delegates shouted her down. Angered, Anthony and a number of the other women left the hall. They organized a committee, with Anthony in the chair, to make arrangements for a separate woman's state temperance association. Thus far events had taken a direction which, however much born of frustration, could only have pleased Cady Stanton. Yet exactly how far toward feminism anger would take the temperance women was uncertain. Only a minority actually followed Anthony out of the hall. Many of these women even objected to the public reading of a letter from Cady Stanton advocating the legalization of divorce for chronic alcoholism.

Cady Stanton's letter to the Albany temperance meeting in 1852 was among her first public espousals of divorce reform, a subject which would shortly become central to her emerging ideology and action. In 1853 she wrote Anthony that she was increasingly convinced that "this whole question of woman's rights turns on the pivot of the marriage relation." Although she did not know "whether the world is quite willing or ready to discuss the question of marriage," she could not avoid it for marriage was, after all, the basic relationship between men and women. Although in a number of western states divorces could be secured for desertion or extreme cruelty, in New York adultery was the only grounds. Among respectable Americans the subject was anathema, and polite society shunned the divorced. Cady Stanton had not mentioned divorce at the Seneca Falls convention. Perhaps emboldened by her success at securing feminist support for suffrage, she decided to propose liberalized divorce legislation. But in an obvious attempt to appeal to the prejudices of temperance women, she proposed that the grounds for divorce be extended only to include heavy and consistent drinking.

In April 1852, at Rochester, New York, Cady Stanton, Anthony, and other women, including woman's rights advocates Lucy Stone, Ernestine Rose, Lucretia Mott, and Martha Wright, established the New York Woman's Temperance Society. Anthony was in ostensible control of the founding meeting: Cady Stanton was elected president and Anthony secretary. This time Cady Stanton was present. Her presidential acceptance speech (delivered in bloomer dress) softened her feminism to appeal to a conservative audience. She stressed two themes: For the majority of her listeners, still supporters of religious benevolence, she declared that ending poverty and the oppression of women was more important than sending missionaries and Bibles to the heathen; to temperance compatriots she stressed the need for divorce for chronic drunkenness. Yet she also declared her intention to address the social ills involved in marriage, prostitution, and the general subjection of women and called on her audience to end their dependency on men and their general "lethargy, the shackles of a false education, customs, and habits."

Yet Cady Stanton had underestimated the conservatism of her audience. Criticism of the speech was overwhelming. The

majority believed that God's promise guaranteed the chris-
tianizing of the world, and they accepted their society's axiom
that marriage was inviolable. A woman with an alcoholic husband must reform him; she had no right to end the relationship. Even Antoinette Brown debated Cady Stanton on the
issue of divorce, which Brown opposed. Over Cady Stanton's
opposition the majority voted to open membership in the organization to men.

After the temperance meeting, Cady Stanton returned to
Seneca Falls. Anthony, appointed state agent of the society,
began her long career as traveling organizer of reform. That
summer she journeyed through New York. Her experiences
convinced her that woman's rights ought to take precedence
over temperance. While attending a state teachers' convention
she found that, although the majority of delegates were
women, none participated in the discussions. Shocked at such
discrimination in a profession she long had practiced, she rose
in the meeting to assail male domination. For a number of
years thereafter, she attended each state teachers' convention
on behalf of woman's equal participation; and generally Cady
Stanton wrote her speeches.

In January 1853, Anthony took another bold step when she
secured a hearing before the legislature and read an appeal,
written by Cady Stanton, advocating legislation either to license and thus to limit the number of liquor outlets in the state
or to allow women to vote on such measures. At subsequent
meetings in New York City sponsored by the men's state organization, outraged conservative temperance advocates again
refused the floor to delegates from the Anthony-Cady Stanton
New York State Woman's Temperance Society. The stage was
set for the final confrontation.

In June 1853, at the first annual meeting of the woman's
state organization, conservative women joined with new male
members to deny Cady Stanton reelection as president. Even
Amelia Bloomer, whom Cady Stanton had carefully cultivated,
now broke with her and remained within the male dominated
society. Cady Stanton was not surprised, but her defeat bore

a painful resemblance to the ouster of women during the 1840 London World Anti-Slavery Convention. Her efforts to radicalize conservative temperance women had failed. Rather than continue their maneuverings among temperance advocates, she and Anthony and the other woman's rights leaders abandoned the organization, which, without their vigorous leadership, soon died. Even *The Lily* lapsed publication in 1856.

Through her brief experiences in temperance and dress reform, Cady Stanton had learned some useful lessons. Although she would later take care to maintain her credibility with conservatives, never again would she attempt to center her feminist activity around their support and the hope of radicalizing them. Rather, in the future she would be drawn to radical groups and radical action. Soon she abandoned all caution in making public her radical views about marital relations. "A multitude of timid, undeveloped men and women, afraid of priests and politicians," she concluded from her experiences in the early 1850s, "are a hindrance rather than a help in any reform." She remembered how Garrison had forced national recognition of the morality of antislavery with a "thoroughly sifted" small group of "picked men and women." Numbers were not necessary; determination and evangelical ability were.

With the failure of the temperance coalition, feminist leaders in New York formed a separate state woman's rights organization, in which Susan Anthony was the guiding force. Beginning in 1854, the state woman's rights convention was held each year in Albany during the legislative session, when lobbying efforts could be mounted. As agent of the organization, Anthony superintended the women who toured the state, speaking and circulating petitions. She herself spent many months on the road. By 1860 the campaign scored its first major success. In that year, the New York legislature gave married women the right to their earnings and equal custody over their children.

In addition to drafting resolutions and writing speeches for Anthony, Cady Stanton's main involvement came in two major speeches. In 1854 she addressed the joint judiciary committees of the legislature in the Senate chambers; in 1860 she spoke before a joint session of the legislature. These appearances marked her growing reputation as a woman's rights orator. Feminists distributed 20,000 copies of her 1854 speech throughout the state. Such acclaim was highly gratifying. But at the same time it made her general isolation in Seneca Falls even harder, particularly after the break with Bloomer. The situation was ripe for the last major crisis in Cady Stanton's mature life and for her final and most radical assertion of independence.

Since moving to Seneca Falls in 1847, Cady Stanton had borne four of her seven children—sons Theodore and Robert and daughters Harriot and Margaret. Pregnancy and childbirth had generally been easy for her, but the last pregnancy in 1859 was extremely difficult. Physical problems forced her to cancel her appearance in a prestigious Boston lecture series, and the withdrawal mortified her because she had always ridiculed the popular argument that pregnancy made public life impossible for women. She developed a serious postpartum depression. In addition, her beloved cousin, Gerrit Smith, spent time in a mental institution that year because of emotional disorientation caused by John Brown's raid on Harper's Ferry, which he had supported financially. Finally, that same year, her adored father died.

In 1859 Cady Stanton was forty-four. Approaching menopause, a condition that her culture viewed as an illness which drained vitality and caused physical and emotional problems, she could not help being apprehensive. Her life thus far had been punctuated by crises: in 1826, when her brother had died; in 1831, after an exposure to Protestant revivalism; in 1840, during her engagement to Henry Stanton; and in 1847, when she and her family had moved to Seneca Falls. She had resolved each crisis through positive action that modified the course of her life.

She responded to the crisis of her middle years in a similar manner. In this case, as in 1847, much of the difficulty focused on her marriage and her desire for an independent life. In

December 1859, she wrote to Anthony that the death of her father, the martyrdom of John Brown, and the breakdown of her cousin all made her regret her "dwarfed womanhood." If only she could be a man, she wrote, so that she might enjoy unlimited freedom. Sometime that year, she decided to make public without reservation her liberal views on divorce, and in 1861, she embarked on the first substantial lecture tour of her career.

In 1860, she startled the tenth National Woman's Rights Convention by introducing resolutions damning current attitudes and laws on marriage and divorce. In an accompanying speech, she called for the recognition of marriage as a simple civil contract, easily dissolved when both partners so decided. For some time liberals in the New York legislature, like liberal legislators in other states, had tried to modify the New York divorce law by adding extreme cruelty, desertion, and alcoholism to adultery as grounds for divorce. Since the early 1850s, woman's rights advocates had privately discussed the need to raise the question of divorce, particularly in terms of a married woman's right to her own body, but none of them had had the nerve to do so publicly. Moreover, the feminist campaign for equal legal rights for women seemed to have succeeded with passage of the 1860 Married Women's Property Act. The time was right, it seemed, to introduce a new woman's rights issue, especially since most feminists expected that suffrage would soon be achieved, probably at the time of the planned revision of the New York state constitution in the mid-1860s.

Cady Stanton had not counted on opposition to her proposals. She later asserted that, had she realized their divisiveness, she might not have introduced them. Many of those present, like Antoinette Brown Blackwell, opposed liberalizing the divorce laws. Many, however, simply wanted to defer a new and controversial issue to a more propitious time. New York City was crowded with reformers and observers of all persuasions who had come to attend the variety of annual meetings, including religious missionary and antislavery, held there in May of each year in what was known as Anniversary Week. Cady Stanton had chosen a time of maximum publicity to introduce her new ideas. The possibility that this publicity might damage woman's rights and even abolitionism in this time of violent sectional controversy fueled the negative reaction she aroused. Wendell Phillips and William Lloyd Garrison, present at the woman's rights meeting, suggested a compromise that, in effect, put off the issue. Since divorce affected men as well as women, they argued, the issue did not properly belong to the woman's rights movement and ought to be taken up in a separate convention. Even Lucy Stone supported their stance. Given such opposition, the convention did not adopt Cady Stanton's resolutions, although the majority refused to expunge them from the minutes, as Phillips had wanted.

Phillips, Garrison, and other abolitionists were already displaying a lack of sensitivity to woman's rights which would become patent after the Civil War. Several months after the 1860 woman's rights convention they pressed Anthony to reveal the hiding place of a Massachusetts woman who had abducted her daughter from her husband in defiance of Massachusetts child custody laws and then come to Anthony for help. To Garrison and Phillips, the fugitive was simply in violation of the law. Her association with Anthony, who since 1857 had worked for antislavery as well as for woman's rights, threatened the abolitionist movement. To Anthony and Cady Stanton, the woman's case was as compelling as that of any runaway slave the abolitionists had harbored—unlawful concealment which they justified because the fugitive slave law was harsh and unjust. Evidence indicated that the husband of Anthony's fugitive wife—himself a Massachusetts state senator —had beaten her when she had challenged him with proof of his infidelity, had taken custody of their children, and had committed her to a mental institution. Cady Stanton and Anthony saw in her plight the predicament of all women. They did not disclose her whereabouts.

Despite their anger at the abolitionist leaders over this case and over divorce reform, Anthony and Cady Stanton agreed with them over the gravity of the national situation. The 1860 presidential election of Abraham Lincoln, a moderate on slavery who might compromise with the South, particularly alarmed them, as it did all Garrisonians. Early in 1861 Cady Stanton addressed the New York Senate Judiciary Committee in support of pending divorce legislation, but thereafter kept silent on the issue for a number of years.

In 1860 Susan Anthony accepted a charge to organize an abolitionist tour in New York State to rouse sentiment for immediate emancipation. She asked Cady Stanton to join the group. Despite the fact that she had small children at home, including a baby, Cady Stanton went on the tour. It was the first time she had left home for a number of weeks on behalf of reform without her children. It was her final act of personal rebellion against her Seneca Falls situation, against her Johnstown family, and against her husband. Publicly, she had declared herself a Garrisonian. Symbolically, she had chosen a course of action which reproduced the abolitionist speaking tours which had brought Henry Stanton his early fame. She even faced hostile crowds, just as her husband had thirty years before. The possibility of civil war created fear and dissension among Americans everywhere, and the abolitionist message, implicitly prowar, elicited violent opposition. In Rochester and Buffalo, angry throngs made so much noise that her speeches could not be heard. In Albany, the Mayor sat on the platform with them, holding a gun in plain view. Police lined the hall inside and out to maintain order.

In 1862 Cady Stanton moved with her family to New York City, where Henry Stanton had secured a position as Deputy Collector of the New York Customs House, a political appointment which finally rewarded his work for the Republican party. Cady Stanton was ready for the move. Her sisters Harriet and Tryphena, with their husbands Daniel Eaton and Edward Bayard, lived in New York City. Above all, the move put her at the center of feminist and reform politics and gave her access to the cultural opportunities she had relished in Boston. With this move to New York City, a new phase of her life had begun.

The Feminist Philosopher

As a REFORMER and public figure, Cady Stanton was first and foremost a feminist. In contrast to Lucy Stone and Antoinette Brown, whose abolitionism predated their feminism and long remained their primary commitment, Cady Stanton became an antislavery activist only when the Civil War impended. She once spent an afternoon in the late 1850s at Lucy Stone's New Jersey home, discussing the oppression of women and Southern slaves. Neither could shake the other's convictions. "Stone felt the slaves' wrongs more deeply than her own," reported Cady Stanton. With irony and insight into her own motivation, she added, "My philosophy was more egotistical." In 1860 she boldly asserted that "the prejudice against sex is more deeply rooted and more unreasonably maintained than that against color."

Her feminism was reinforced by her love of speculation, which drew her toward a search for the underlying principles of human and social behavior. She once wrote that she liked Herbert Spencer because he taught readers "to lose sight of ourselves and our burdens." Her need to escape from the pressures of personal and political confrontation in the woman's movement through philosophical speculation was as strong as her satisfaction in activism. As it was, she carried on the tradition of feminist intellectualism which Margaret Fuller had begun earlier in the century and which Charlotte Perkins Gilman would continue in the early twentieth century. She was the foremost American woman intellectual of her generation.

As a theorist, however, Cady Stanton was largely un-
heralded outside of feminist circles. She never wrote a full-
length analytical work. Shortly after the Seneca Falls
convention, she wrote Lucretia Mott of her intention to write
a woman's rights treatise on the order of those by Mary Wollstonecraft and Sarah Grimké, but she never completed the
project. Her only long writings were an autobiography, *Eighty
years and More,* published in 1898, and two edited compila-
tions, the multivolume *History of Woman Suffrage,* published in
the 1880s, and *The Woman's Bible,* published in the 1890s.
Speeches and articles comprised the bulk of her work. Furthermore, she was never part of an intellectual community. She
read and wrote at home, in isolation; and the demands of
domesticity, of social life, and of reform work restricted her
time for analysis and writing.

Cady Stanton's central aim was to alter attitudes toward
women. To serve this end, she turned particularly to oratory
and journalism, forms of expression whose goals of enlightenment and persuasion are best served by simple argument without intellectual trappings. A voracious reader, she linked her
feminist premises to whatever popular ideas—like republicanism, or social Darwinism, or the notion of woman's moral
superiority—might strike a positive response in her audience
and become a vehicle for persuasion. She wrote quickly and,
like any able polemicist, did not always successfully eliminate
contradictions. Her speeches and articles often contained
varying points of view, and this lack of consistency makes her
writings both challenging and difficult to analyze. Her friend
and most insightful biographer, Laura Curtis Bullard, put it
well: "Like any speaker or journalist, her finest productions
have been those of an ephemeral type."

Cady Stanton's central concerns—the behavior of men and
women, marriage, the family—had always been peripheral to
the main emphasis of the Western philosophical tradition. Nor
were the suffragists of the early twentieth century entirely fair
in representing Cady Stanton's views. Their energies fastened
on a single reform; her grandchildren's generation often re-

duced her complex stance to a simple focus on suffrage. Theodore Tilton, a friend and fellow reformer, realized the interdependent role of suffrage in her thought, and put it well in an 1895 tribute. To Cady Stanton, Tilton wrote, suffrage had been more a means than an end; its lack more a symbol of woman's degradation than its major cause. Indeed, as Tilton realized, woman's suffrage had never been more important to her than such concerns as divorce, coeducation, or changing basic attitudes about men and women.

Throughout her career, the sources of Cady Stanton's philosophy lay both in her extensive reading and her own experience. Her ideology was intertwined with her autobiography. Her life was a primary source for her ideas, which in turn influenced her actions. Fully developed by the 1860s, the essential lines of her thought remained fixed until the last two decades of her life. Her dedication to feminist individualism was a constant theme, as was her belief in the efficacy of education and the superior value of coeducation over single-sex education. She never abandoned her support of woman suffrage or her belief that reform in marital relationships was the key to human progress.

In the 1860s, a period of frustrating confrontation in her public life, she enunciated the popular doctrine of woman's moral superiority which she had earlier criticized, and she showed interest in socialist theories about class conflict and worker exploitation. Again in the 1860s, after reading some of the anthropological and sociological systems builders of the period, she formulated a feminist theory of historical development. Before the 1890s these were the only substantial modifications in her ideology.

The initial intellectual sources of Cady Stanton's ideas lay in the works of earlier feminist theorists like Mary Wollstonecraft and Margaret Fuller and in the natural rights and republican theories of the American Enlightenment. Wollstonecraft and Fuller provided her with the ammunition to attack prevailing notions of male superiority and to advance the strikingly modern argument that whatever differences existed between men and women were cultural and not innate. In Cady Stanton's view, women possessed the same range of abilities as men. Even though most men were taller and stronger than most women, many men were not. Napoleon Bonaparte and Aaron Burr, for example, had been short and slight. There were cultures in which heavy labor was deemed woman's work as much as man's. Among Tartar tribes, she contended, women rode horses, hunted wild animals, and fought in battle alongside their men. Croatian and Walachian women performed all the heavy agricultural labor for their society. In the United States, if women were more emotional, less intelligent, or more prone to illness than men it was because society had made them so by denying them an education, a profession, exercise, and sensible clothing.

There was therefore no justification for denying women the freedoms extended to all by natural right and republican theory. "We hold these truths to be self-evident: that all men and women are created equal," Cady Stanton had written in the 1848 Seneca Falls declaration. The heirs of the Revolution, whatever their political stripe or ideological commitment, whether Federalist or Republican, Democrat or Whig, had violated their principles by creating and accepting in the private sphere of male-female relations the very tyranny of one group over another they feared in the public arena. Cady Stanton questioned not only the Jacksonian commitment to democratic equality but also the sincerity of the founding fathers of the nation who had created an egalitarian government and constructed a system of constitutional checks and balances to thwart majority tyranny and democratic excess only to create an "aristocracy of sex." Jacksonian democracy rested on the subordination of women, she believed; American republicans had established a dictatorship over women in violation of their own republicanism.

The "aristocracy of sex" was more threatening to human development than any hierarchy based on class or color. There was not one evil, she wrote, that could not be traced to the degradation of women. The sexual system had made women a special caste within society—a group whose similar concerns transcended all divisions by class, family, or ethnicity. Against conservatives who argued that women were favored and protected by husbands and fathers, Cady Stanton stressed the harsh costs of male domination. She emphasized not only the detrimental effects of legal and political discrimination but also the social suffering of women who lived in poverty because of employment and wage discrimination, or who were forced into prostitution, or who were prey to the physical violence of alcoholic or brutal husbands. "As my heart swells with pride to behold woman in the highest walks of literature and art," she wrote, "it grows big enough to take in those who are bleeding in the dust." The "aristocracy of sex" had increased masculine arrogance and led to widespread abuses of the power it conferred. Rape, prostitution, and wife beating were among its most egregious by-products. "Who ever saw a human being that would not abuse unlimited power?" she asked, her own debt to republicanism clearly showing through.

The aristocracy of sex was as injurious to its masters as to its subordinates. It supported a social order as damaging for men as for women. Prostitution, for example, benefited no one. "Go into the streets of your cities at the midnight hour, and there behold those whom God meant to be Queens in the moral universe, giving your sons and mine their first lessons in infamy and vice." The aristocracy of sex was omnipresent. Cady Stanton often exaggerated the evils she described in order to emphasize them. She was well aware that many women did not think they were oppressed. In exasperation, she pointed out that sexual prejudice was easily overlooked because it was everywhere, in the attitude of every man, in every book and magazine. It was an integral part of common speech in such pejorative categorizations as "there's woman's work for you" or "there's a woman's judgment," and in the common derisive descriptions of effeminate men as "Miss Nancy's" and "Old Grannys."

The aristocracy of sex included not only well-to-do but also working-class men. Indeed, she believed that violent crimes against women were usually committed by working-class men. In Seneca Falls, women in the Irish community near her home often called her out at night to stop drunken husbands from beating their children. Her residence in New York City in the 1860s confirmed these sentiments. Refined sensualism was a crime common among wealthy men; rape and wife beating were working-class crimes. "As you go down and down in the scale of manhood," she wrote, "the idea strengthens and strengthens, at every step, that woman was created for no higher purpose than to gratify the lust of man." Moreover, lack of education made effective action by workers impossible. "The great battle for the laborer must be fought for him by the educated classes," she wrote, "just as for the slave."

Such attitudes clouded her usually libertarian views toward workers and blacks, whom she included in the general indictment. In later years she demanded educational qualifications for voting and categorized Irish and black males according to ethnic stereotypes. In the last decade of her life she supported American imperialism on the grounds of Anglo-Saxon superiority. Yet she often wrote with passion of the ills workers and blacks suffered. "In full enjoyment of your blessings," she told a middle-class audience in 1868, "look around in the filthy lanes and bystreets of all our cities, the laboring multitudes ragged, starving, packed in dingy cellars, and garrets. Is it right that a large majority . . . should suffer . . . that a small minority may enjoy all life's blessings and benefits?" Her commitment to abolitionism and to workers' rights was secondary to her feminism but was nonetheless strong. In 1868, in 1871, and in the 1890s, Cady Stanton explored the possibility of a coalition among feminists, workers, blacks, and radicals. Still, she most often argued that a coalition of women of all classes, rather than of the radicals and the dispossessed alone, would effect any ultimate social transformation.

In keeping with the individualistic and evangelical spirit of the age, Cady Stanton also held that individual reform and regeneration, as well as political and feminist coalition, was a central strategy for social change. Although she worked within the woman's movement throughout her career, in later years such institutional involvement was not her primary commitment. "It is not in conventions . . . that our best work begins," she wrote as early as 1851. "The radical reform must start in our homes, in our nurseries, in ourselves." Her own experience led her to this prescription. In Seneca Falls she had been a homeopathic doctor and psychological counselor, ministering to individuals in distress. The development of her children had been as important to her as any ideological issue. She had struggled for years to understand the nature of sin and salvation in relation to her own life.

Her education as well as her experience led her to emphasize the rights and responsibilities of individuals more than those of society or the state. The emphasis on self-reliance and self-control in her writings echoed childhood teachings about the primacy of personal piety and repression of self. The classics, with their emphasis on moral education through the study of individual example, formed the core of the curriculum at both Johnstown Academy and Troy Seminary. What interested her most in her legal studies, she asserted, was equity law, which, she believed, dealt with the reconciliation of the rights of the individual with those of society. "I place man above all governments, all institutions," she proclaimed.

Contemporary intellectual currents also prompted her to center her philosophy around the concept of humans as individuals. Ralph Waldo Emerson, who stressed self-knowledge through contemplation, was one of her favorite authors. She rejected the faith of Charles Grandison Finney, but she preserved his emphasis on individual moral regeneration. Phrenologists, no less than Emerson or Finney, focused on individual health and happiness. Finally, natural rights and liberal philosophers stressed the individual. She praised John Stuart Mill's *On the Subjection of Women* (1869) as the best treatise yet written on the subject of woman's oppression, which Mill traced not to law or society, but primarily to individual relationships between men and women.

Despite her emphasis on the individual, Cady Stanton believed that society was an organic whole so interconnected that the good of one individual would contribute to the betterment of all. It was a notion congenial to an age of optimism in which populations were small and group revivalism common, where radicals and reformers regarded human nature as basically good and inevitably receptive to doctrines of social change. Cady Stanton thought that the frequent debates among reformers about "whether it is better to sacrifice the few to the many or the many to the few," to concentrate on individual reformation or general social change, were unnecessary. "If we obey the laws of our being there need be no such thing as sacrifice at all, for in all cases the highest good of one is the highest good of all, and the highest good of all does not require the sacrifice of one individual."

Cady Stanton's individualism was central to the independent stance she adopted throughout her career as a feminist and a reformer. It lay behind her disagreement, at least into the 1860s, with the common feminist argument that women, equal to men in most ways, were superior to them in morality. The belief in woman's moral superiority drew on the righteous anger of an oppressed minority, and it mirrored the popular belief that woman's natural moral endowments were the necessary support of the family, the school, and the republic itself. With some exasperation Cady Stanton wrote in 1856 that she was just about the only woman's rights advocate who still held that men and women had similar natures.

Yet even in the 1850s Cady Stanton found the argument for superiority appealing, particularly when it applied to women as mothers. In her experience maternity had been a "natural joy." Attracted to the contemporary celebration of motherhood, she often vaunted the special ability of the "republican mother" to teach her family the virtues of simplicity and benevolence. "As mothers of the race," she wrote, "there is a spiritual insight, a divine creative power that belongs to women." On one occasion she advocated giving every mother title to a dwelling as a way of eliminating poverty and of insuring the moral education of the family.

Yet she continued to have difficulties with the argument for woman's superiority. In public statements she often used it with calculation and for its resonance among her audiences. In 1867 she stated that she had adopted it partly out of expediency, because she was tired of battling conservatives who refused to accede to the equality of the sexes but accepted woman's moral superiority. Moreover, her many negative experiences with women made it impossible for her to accept the idea completely. She often criticized women as severely as men. Her diatribes against wealthy women who lived for fashion and display off the labor of hardworking husbands equaled her most vituperative antimale outbursts. These women constituted an "aristocracy of women" as destructive as the male aristrocracy of sex.

In despairing moments she regarded women, because of their sycophantic, slavelike behavior toward men and particularly toward their husbands, as the source of human ills rather than as humankind's potential benefactors. Dependency, she thought, made many women incapable of direct, honest behavior, and their children imitated their ways. "Just so long as women have no individual aims, desires, opinions, and purposes in life, but secure their ends by echoing, wheedling and managing men," she wrote, "your men will be of the same plastic character, governed by policy rather than principle, led by the nose, by wily politicians." In the kind of contradiction characteristic of her thought, she often criticized the contemporary cult of motherhood, to which she was committed elsewhere in her writings, and counseled women not to marry until they were older and independent. "Womanhood is the great fact, wifehood and motherhood its incidents," a favorite aphorism, reflected her concern over the dependency of married women as well as her desire to justify the independent course she had herself taken in 1861.

Cady Stanton was further aware that cultural attitudes often dictated individual behavior, that men and women were not entirely to blame for their behavior. "We are all what law, custom, and public sentiment have made us," she wrote. In-

deed, Cady Stanton's later theorizing about woman's superiority was generally encompassed within the larger context of
what she saw as the complementary nature of the sexes. Ideally
women embodied peace and love and men positive energy and
rationality. But because society was defective, women were
petty and men destructively aggressive. Politics, morality, and
society needed a balance between the ideal masculine and
feminine elements. "Just as the constituent elements of nitro-
gen and oxygen make the necessary atmosphere in which man
can breath and live," she wrote in the 1860s, "so are the male
and female elements in their true proportion necessary for our
moral life." Even when she adopted the argument that human
history had originated in peaceful, democratic, matriarchal
societies which were destroyed by aggressive, dictatorial, patriarchal ones, she contended that the final goal of history
would not be a return to the rule of women but rather to the
"amphiarchate," the combined rule of men and women.

Like many liberal reformers of her age, disenchanted by the
notable failures of religious missions, temperance crusades,
penal reform, and pauper relief, Cady Stanton looked to universal education as a cure for social ills. Early and correct
schooling held out the prospect of hope because the behavior
of the young was pliable, their minds still open. She favored
educating men and women together from the earliest years
through college. In that way, they would share the same tasks,
learn mutual respect, see the fallacy of the idea of separate
spheres, and then conclude marriages based on true intellectual and spiritual companionship. Her arguments for coeducation often drew on her own experience of easy comradeship
with the boys at Johnstown Academy in contrast to the artifi-
cial, sexually charged atmosphere of the all-female world of
Emma Willard's school. She praised western colleges, in which
coeducation was the rule, because "boys and girls would learn
to regard each other as equals" and would participate in "the
higher pleasure of a mutual flow and interflow of brain forces,
galvanizing both into grander thoughts and nobler aspirations." She criticized eastern colleges for segregating the

sexes. Nevertheless she sent her daughters to Vassar, although Harriot Stanton wanted to attend Cornell, the first important eastern experiment in coeducation.

The central themes of Cady Stanton's feminist position and her characteristically pragmatic and polemical presentation of them were in full evidence in her 1854 speech before the judiciary committees of the New York legislature. She considered it one of her finest addresses. She began by demanding full legal and social rights for women, on behalf of the "daughters of the revolutionary heroes of '76." She expressed amazement that the legislators, committed to democracy and republicanism, could have willingly brought into being a sexual aristocracy that placed "the ignorant and the vulgar above the educated and refined—the alien and the ditch-digger above the authors and poets." She detailed the specifics of woman's oppression, focusing in this case on the "slave status" of married women, whose husbands could even administer physical punishment to them under the law, and on the legal exclusion of women from juries. "Shall an erring woman be dragged before a bar of grim-visaged judges, lawyers, and jurors, there to be grossly questioned in public on subjects which women scarce breathe in secret to one another?"

Even the legislators' own daughters, "lapped amidst luxuries which your indulgences spreads," might fall prey to these laws. For particular vituperation she singled out the laws which gave fathers exclusive rights over children. These laws violated the "sacred relation" between mother and child, gave additional strength to immoral male culture with its gambling and saloons, and simply gave men too much power. The existing child custody laws supported the horror of child prostitution. "By the abuse of this absolute power, he may bind his daughter to the owner of a brothel, and by the degradation of his child, supply his daily wants."

Referring to Enlightenment theory, Cady Stanton argued that by right women were owed equality under the law. Since men and women had similar natures, there was no justification for special laws for women. But a hint of the belief in woman's moral superiority infused her argument that equal rights were crucial to bettering society. "It is folly to talk of a mother moulding the character of her son, when all mankind, backed up by law and public sentiments, conspire to destroy her influence." The New York legislators could hardly disagree. Immediately she expanded the argument into the public arena: "Woman's moral power ought to speak, not only in the home but also through the ballot box." But Cady Stanton was careful not to alarm the legislators nor to threaten their personal interests. Woman's voting, she contended, would operate primarily to reform young men through the regulation of saloons and gambling halls, "which lure our youth on to excessive indulgence and destruction."

In 1854 Cady Stanton had not yet accepted the notion that men and women were different by nature. Nor for a decade would she completely work out her ideas about the complementary nature of the sexes. This speech did not mention coeducation. But she did contend that the feminists represented the majority of women: those who supported themselves, their husbands, and their children; the 50,000 wives of alcoholics (by Cady Stanton's count); women in workhouses, poorhouses, and prisons. "Who are they that we do not represent? But a small class of the fashionable butterflies, who, through the short summer days, seek the sunshine and the flowers; but . . . the hoary frosts of winter will soon chase all these away; then they, too, will need and seek protection."

In her 1854 speech Cady Stanton referred to but did not dwell on those ideas about marriage and divorce which she had publicly expressed to the temperance women and which would soon dominate her ideology and action. To the legislators she told the story of "noble, virtuous, well-educated mothers" who had abandoned alcoholic husbands but who, under New York law, were denied custody of their children. One of these women, who possessed "a grandeur of attitude and manner worthy the noble Roman matron in the palmiest days of the Republic," had told her: "I would rather never see my child again, than be the medium to hand down the low animal nature of its father, to stamp degradation on the brow of another innocent being."

By 1860 Cady Stanton announced her conviction that the marriage question lay "at the foundation of all human progress." The aristocracy of sex had its most immediate domination within marriage, for law and custom gave each man the right to tyrannize his wife. Property laws might be liberalized and the vote achieved, but these gains would be negligible if marriage and the family were not transformed. In the family, the "miniature of the state," adult attitudes were formed. It could be the source of a virtuous citizenry or of "domestic infidelity, social duplicity, religious hypocrisy, and political trickery."

Her concern for the family extended even to the unborn who would comprise the next generation. Parents played a crucial role in the emotional and mental makeup of their children, she believed. In the first place, the pregnant woman's emotions, no matter how momentary, passed on to the developing fetus. "During the nine months of prenatal life," she wrote, "they are stamping every thought and feeling of their minds on the plastic beings." She attributed her own adult fear of cats to her mother's having been frightened by a cat when carrying her. During her own pregnancies she followed her beliefs by resting, carefully exercising, listening to music, and pursuing her woman's rights activities in a moderate manner.

She went even further. In her view the mood and condition of the parents at conception affected the child's personality. The primary danger here was that alcoholic fathers would produce deformed children. Yet even unhappily married partners might produce weak or disturbed infants. "Any woman sacrifices her claims to virtue and nobility," she wrote sternly, "who consents to live in the relation of wife with any man whom she has ceased to love and respect."

Such theories were primitive versions of late nineteenth- and early twentieth-century eugenics, which held that selective breeding could produce a better race of human beings. Many contemporary marriage and child care manuals lent respectability to the idea, a common folk belief, that the mother's actions and emotions during pregnancy influenced the fetus. For phrenologists the notion of prenatal influence was a logical corollary of the belief in the interdependence of emotional and physiological development. Moreover, hereditarian thought provided an explanation for the disappointing behavior of Cady Stanton's two eldest sons. Not until some time after the 1845 birth of her third son, Gerrit, she contended, had she adopted these naturalistic theories and begun to apply them to her own conduct.

Cady Stanton's argument for biological influence contradicted her theories about cultural conditioning and disputed the Lockean tradition to which many contemporary feminist writers were committed. John Locke, the seminal seventeenth-century British philosopher, had argued that the infant was born with no emotional or behavior predispositions, that the human mind was a "blank slate" at birth. As a consequence, men and women were products of their environing culture, not of inherent predispositions. Although in 1852 Cady Stanton criticized Locke for failing to realize that prenatal influences were paramount in infant personality and in 1868 argued that morality was hereditary, she never fully explained the relative weight to be assigned to inherited and cultural factors. Here as elsewhere, she did not concern herself with contradictions.

Cady Stanton recognized that men and women shared the responsibility for producing defective offspring, yet she usually held men to blame because of their natural propensity to indulge what she saw as their animal appetites, particularly for liquor and sex. In her opinion marriage was often little more than licensed prostitution. Even when she stressed the equality of men and women, she held women naturally superior to men in their ability to control their sexuality. Cady Stanton did not condemn sex, and she acknowledged that women could enjoy sexual relations. But she argued that the greatest human satisfactions stemmed from moral and intellectual activities and that overindulgence in sexuality, largely at the bidding of men, was detrimental to women and to marriage. In her lectures and writings, Cady Stanton did not discuss specific birth control techniques, taking care, as she once explained, not to offend audiences on this sensitive issue or to run the risk of possible prosecution. Yet like many contemporary advocates of "enlightened motherhood," she seemed to advocate abstinence as a primary method.

Cady Stanton's views on sex reflected the prejudices of her age. One of her major objections to the women's fashions of her day was that the accentuation of the bosom and hips then popular advertised woman's sexuality over her mind and spirit; and she championed the bloomer dress because it was designed for convenience and not to attract men. Indeed, she criticized low-necked gowns, the tights worn by women dancers on stage, and the sensual posturings of the celebrated courtesan-actresses Lola Montez and Adah Isaacs Mencken.

Although she never used the term, Cady Stanton's goal was the single standard of morality, a byword among late-nineteenth-century feminists determined to end prostitution and the double standard by mobilizing women to assume responsibility for their sexual conduct and by persuading men to adopt woman's norms of moderation and self-control. After an 1871 speech in San Francisco, "Marriage and Motherhood," delivered before an audience of 600 from which men and reporters were barred, listeners questioned her closely. A reporter who gained entrance by dressing as a woman published the exchange. Question: "How can we follow your advice and keep from having babies?" Answer: "Woman must be at all times the sovereign of her body." Question: "What are we to do when men don't agree?" Answer: "The men must be educated up to the higher civilization as well as the women. The same force that governs the passions can be controlled and directed into the brain power and result in great deeds." She counseled her son Theodore, when in college, to "exercise with dumbbells" rather than visit the "ordinary young girls."

To Cady Stanton a reform in marital relations was crucial

not only for individual fulfillment but also for the future of the race. "Feeble, indifferent, joyless, discordant unions" were observable everywhere, mere "physical unions, in which woman consents to hand down, with no feelings of guilt or sin, the odious moral and physical deformities and diseases of any man whom accident or necessity may have induced her to marry." Because the children born to them would almost inevitably be defective, they were the cause of "disease, vice, crime, the idiot, the deaf, the dumb. . . . All special reforms are hopeless, surface work . . . and there can be no vital change until we understand and observe the immutable laws that govern the most sacred of relations."

The marriage state was to be improved first by allowing the easy termination of unsuccessful unions. As early as 1852 Cady Stanton called for liberalized divorce laws and sought to enlist others behind her efforts. Second, it was imperative that women accept her eugenic theories, that they practice her form of "enlightened motherhood," although she at first hesitated to stress this reform publicly for fear of shocking her contemporaries and losing their support. Finally, she emphasized the need to change women's attitudes about society and about men, but especially about themselves. Women as well as men were contributing to their children's deficiencies. Heavy corseting, sedentary living without exercise, and intellectual laziness were as hard on the unborn infant as on the mother. It was impossible "to work out any general reform in any department, until we can raise up a new race of women." The crusade which she envisioned, centered on revolutionizing the minds of American women and focused on the message of birth control, became her chief reform activity in her later career.

Cady Stanton not only emphasized individual relationships in her feminist thought but she also searched for the underlying laws governing nature and society in order to understand the future. Her early and continuing interest in eugenic theory was part of this quest. She came to intellectual maturity in an age when romantic philosophers and utopian socialists were producing large-scale theories of historical and social development. She participated fully in her age's belief in progress. Utopianism and an interest in systems building was part of her ideology. "The future [is] glorious to those who see a fixed law governing equally mind, morals, and matter," she wrote in 1866. "What a grand philosophy of life such men as Herbert Spencer . . . are . . . opening to our minds . . . in the onward march of the race."

In her search she was influenced by the natural law and natural right theories of Enlightenment philosophy which implied the existence of an underlying scheme of human development. In addition, she was particularly influenced by three nineteenth-century systems builders: Herbert Spencer, Auguste Comte, and Johann J. Bachofen. None were feminists. She criticized Spencer harshly for his eventual conclusions about woman's supposed evolutionary inferiority and Comte for his belief that domesticity was woman's proper role. But she also found elements in their thought which legitimated her own theories and thus astutely linked her views with the main tradition of Western social philosophy.

Cady Stanton could hardly ignore Herbert Spencer, the English thinker whose voluminous writings put evolutionary theory into social terms. Spencer gave the final blow to the dogmas of revealed religion that had so troubled her. His belief that humanity's development was inevitably progressive gave her own utopianism scientific authority. Although she overlooked Spencer's contempt for the poor and his belief that the state ought in no way to interfere with evolutionary process, his emphasis on the rights of the individual matched her own libertarianism as well as her belief that the appropriate agents of change were individuals operating according to the voluntary principle. She particularly welcomed Spencer's stress on individual discipline and self-control. "Spencer is one of my favorite authors," she wrote in 1870, citing her agreement with his thesis that "general character can only become better by a steady improvement in the system of education and by discipline."

Auguste Comte provided more direct support for her feminist utopianism than had Spencer. Comte discerned a complex, three-stage system of development both in the history of society and of human thought. The first stage was ruled by religion. Dogma and ritual solidified society; the characteristic mode of thought was theological. The second stage Comte called metaphysical; secularism overtook religion, and formal, philosophical thought focused on abstract phenomena. The final stage, not yet attained, Comte termed positivistic; philosophic inquiry would center directly on human and social experience, and new forms of piety would emerge, constituting a religion of humanity. Comte's system mirrored Cady Stanton's intellectual development from a thinking person bound by religion to an emancipated philosopher and social theorist. But what especially impressed her was Comte's argument that women were to be the agents for effecting his third, positivistic stage and especially for bringing the religion of humanity into being.

Further substantiation for Cady Stanton's feminist view of past and future came from Johann J. Bachofen, whose *Mother Right* dated from 1861. Based on his reading of the anthropological record of primitive people, Bachofen argued that a prehistoric age of unregulated sexual relationship had been followed by a second, matriarchal period in which women were dominant, and a third, patriarchal age, still in existence, in which men were supreme. Cady Stanton focused on the age of matriarchy, which she interpreted as a golden age of peace and plenty. Women, because of their maternal instincts and their need for self-preservation during pregnancy and lactation, had then domesticated agriculture, created stable homes and families, and laid the basis of education, literature, and the arts. Men had finally asserted authority only through their greater willingness to use force and their invention of superior weapons. In opposition to male anthropologists who argued that patriarchy was the highest stage in the inevitably progressive evolution of civilization, Cady Stanton viewed it as the source of tyranny, wars, and general social ills.

Anthropological theories of matriarchy provided the foundations for a feminist interpretation of the course of human history. By Cady Stanton's calculations, they also disproved one of the central arguments for woman's subordination throughout history, the "curse of Eve," a belief older than Christianity. Eve allegedly brought sin into the world because of taking the apple from the serpent in the Garden of Eden and giving it to Adam. She presumably then incurred the more severe punishment, including menstruation, the pain of childbirth, and general inferiority to man. Cady Stanton's interpretation of the matriarchate not only made the Eve story unlikely but also implied that women could, in the future as in the past, create harmonious and productive societies and bring utopia into being.

Cady Stanton was not influenced by Karl Marx despite her occasional economic radicalism and the fact that in 1871 her feminist associate, Victoria Woodhull, published the first American translation of Marx's *Communist Manifesto* (1848) in her *Woodhull and Claflin's Weekly*. Perhaps Marx's theories of class development and conflict left no impression on Cady Stanton because of his general silence on gender divisions in history. Or she may have disliked his criticism of Robert Owen and Charles Fourier, with whose utopian socialism she was familiar both in its theoretical formulation and in the many communitarian societies which had been established in the United States.

Indeed, the "associationist" theories she enunciated in the 1890s drew directly from Owen and Fourier, and in the 1840s and 1850s she toyed with the idea of joining a commune, following the example of a number of friends and reformers. Even Theodore Weld and Angelina Grimké Weld for a few years in the 1850s lived in a New Jersey communitarian society. So intense at times was Cady Stanton's immediate utopian inclination that Anthony worried she might abandon the woman's movement. Her communitarianism had its roots in European social philosophy and in native utopian soil. In addition, in keeping with the mixture of abstract reasoning and personal experience that characterized her thought, her personal discontent at the burden of domesticity also made communitarian societies attractive. They held out the promise not only of social reform but also of "a more harmonious domestic life."

Yet Cady Stanton did not act on her leanings toward communitarianism. Her belief in individualism was too strong, her commitment to feminism too powerful. Theories that traced oppression to the economic order or the class structure intrigued her, and in the 1890s they would play a particularly powerful role in her thought. But above all she believed that woman's oppression was the basic issue and that women were to be the central agents in the social transformations to whose establishment she devoted her life.

In her attitudes about divorce and the general oppression of women, in her communitarianism, Cady Stanton was radical for her age. Few feminists have gone beyond her vision of the amphiarchate: an androgynous society in which roles and responsibilities are assigned by ability and interest and not by sex, in which power is shared equally by men and women, and in which all sex stereotyping is eliminated in the raising of children. Cady Stanton realized the radical implications of such ideas when she wrote in 1868 that it was not the ballot alone that women needed, but, instead, "a revolution in society, politics, and religion."

Nevertheless, Cady Stanton abjured revolutionary tactics and chose to adopt moderate strategies for change. Until late in life she did not take part in the protests against taxation and voting which Lucy Stone, Susan Anthony, and others led. She never followed Garrison in his denunciations of the Constitution. In 1866 she herself ran for a seat in the House of Representatives. When in the 1860s she made tentative moves toward a coalition of workers, women, and blacks, she con-

ceived it as a party of reform, not of revolution. Stirring, revolutionary rhetoric came easily to her pen, but such rhetoric was
in keeping with her self-image as a daughter of the revolution
which, in fact, had brought the nation into being.

Her views on sexuality, on the centrality of motherhood, and
on the inevitability of utopia reflected nineteenth-century patterns of thought. In 1871 Cady Stanton visited the cooperative
community of Greeley, Colorado, named for Horace Greeley.
Hearing her speak for the first time, the adolescent son of the
colony's founder penned a brief but striking description of
her, noting the mixture of traditionalism and radicalism that
characterized her remarks. He wrote of "the great Catholic
soul of Mrs. Stanton, who was long years ahead of her time."
Yet the past and the present, as well as the future, were intertwined in the impression she conveyed. "She seemed to live
in several centuries at once." As fully as she transcended her
age, she was also its product.

V

Radicalism and
The Revolution
1862–1869

THE PLACE where she lived always played an important role in Cady Stanton's life. Her small town upbringing had stimulated independence and sensitivity to injustice. Provincial Seneca Falls, after cosmopolitan Boston, had triggered her involvement in woman's rights. New York City had no less an impact. After a year in Brooklyn, she and her family moved to west forty-fifth street in Manhattan, then near the outskirts of the city but close to Broadway, the central thoroughfare. Residence in the nation's largest city allowed Cady Stanton once again to indulge her love for lectures and the theater. But she also directly confronted social problems like poverty and crime that seemed more concentrated in New York City than anywhere else. The problems of urban women—prostitution, rape, infanticide—engaged her attention and ultimately deepened her feminist radicalism. Initially they were a spur to continuing her public career on behalf of women.

In the midst of the Civil War, women everywhere engaged in war work and assumed public roles. With men in the army and their jobs vacant, women found employment as government clerks, hospital nurses, and salespeople, positions formerly reserved for men. They founded benevolent organizations to raise money for the Union army, and they established hospitals. In 1861 they brought into being the Sanitary Commission, a national agency established under government charter to coordinate all war relief operations, to provide for nurses, hospitals, and ambulance service, to gather vital statistics, and to inspect the sanitary facilities of army camps.

The achievements of benevolent women, generally conservative on woman's rights, offered a challenge to activists who had honored abolitionist entreaties that they suspend woman's rights agitation until the war was won and slavery ended. This generous policy proved disastrous for the woman's rights cause. With feminist organizations disbanded and their activities in abeyance, conservatives easily repealed feminist gains. In 1862, for example, the New York legislature rescinded most of the 1860 Married Women's Property Act, and there was little public outcry.

Between 1863 and 1869 Cady Stanton, in tandem with Anthony, moved boldly to redress the situation. Rarely did others take the initiative away from them. They created an impressive number of organizations: in 1863 the Loyal National Woman's League; in 1864 the American Equal Rights Association; in 1868 the Workingwoman's Association and the Woman's Suffrage Association of America; in 1869 the National Woman Suffrage Association. Yet the very number of their endeavors indicated their underlying indecision over what course to follow. These were confusing years. The emotionalism of war and Reconstruction was intensified by Lincoln's assassination, Southern intransigence over black rights, and scandals in government and business. Older reform leaders were retiring; a new generation of reformers was emerging.

Above all, abolitionists, Republicans, and even allies like Lucy Stone one by one deserted woman's suffrage to work for the enactment of black male suffrage. Incredulous, Cady Stanton watched former allies become bitter critics as the pervasive sense of crisis caused a hardening of individual positions. To a large extent, the many organizations she and Anthony initiated were attempts to master a continuously shifting situation.

Yet Cady Stanton became increasingly angry as former friends abandoned feminist positions they previously had held.

A growing distaste for the violence of the city also fueled her wrath. In 1863 destructive riots over the enforcement of an unpopular draft lottery threatened her house and family. In 1864 a disastrous personal experience compounded her anger: Henry Stanton was accused of taking bribes at the New York Customs House. Cady Stanton believed that Republican party jealousy and the desire to conceal the real sources of corruption motivated the attack. She refused to accept the clear evidence that her son Daniel, whom Stanton had unwisely hired as an assistant, was guilty. Rather she blamed the "sons of Adam" in the rotten Republican administration "under which we may write justice obsolete."

For her own emotional life, the anger of these years was positive. In 1860 she had weathered the difficulties of her middle years to emerge self-reliant. Stressful situations now produced anger and action, not depression. Yet her tendency to take immediate action became too automatic; she simply did not take sufficient time to weigh alternatives or to consider outcomes. In the 1850s she had quickly abandoned dress and temperance reform when they did not serve her purposes; in the 1860s and 1870s she would follow a similar pattern with worker and radical politics. Even her shifts from suffrage to divorce reform and eventually to anticlericalism were in many ways examples of inconsistency and political naiveté. "I was always courageous in saying what I saw to be true," she wrote in her autobiography, "for the simple reason that I never dreamed of opposition. What seemed to me to be right I thought must be equally plain to all other rational beings." This is the statement of an enthusiast, not a politician or planner, and it overlooks the fact that Cady Stanton occasionally abandoned a cause when strong opposition emerged.

Yet her dilemma was that of any proponent of a minority, radical position, faced with a situation in which almost any strategy is doomed. Both her boldness and her naive enthusiasm for trying a variety of approaches were apparent in her 1866 campaign for a seat in the House of Representatives from New York City. She decided hastily upon the effort, after realizing that, although women could not vote, the law did not prohibit them from seeking office. Her campaign was neither extensive nor effective, and out of 20,000 votes, she received twenty-four. Her only real impact was symbolic: she had become the first woman in the history of the nation to run for Congress.

But the campaign had an additional significance, suggestive of her future actions: During it she had operated independently of Susan Anthony. Anthony not only lived with her during her years in New York City but also was her constant companion in reform. Before the war Cady Stanton had been the senior partner in defining policy and planning strategy. But Anthony had opposed the policy of suspending woman's rights activities during the war, and Cady Stanton, deciding in retrospect that her friend had been correct, determined to defer more often to Anthony. By the mid-1860s their relationship reached an equality which would be maintained through difficult years of conflict with abolitionists and reconstitution of the woman's movement, until Anthony's growing authority and their differing strategies caused a rift in the relationship which was one factor behind the independent course Cady Stanton eventually took.

In May 1863 Cady Stanton and Anthony founded the Woman's Loyal National League. Its purpose was to mount a campaign to petition Congress to emancipate southern slaves. Union morale was low, and Lincoln's recent Emancipation Proclamation, which gave the erroneous impression of freeing all southern slaves, actually applied only to blacks in territories occupied by Union armies. Honoring their commitment to the abolitionists to forego feminism, Cady Stanton and Anthony mobilized the prewar woman's rights forces for the cause of blacks. But feminism was not far from their minds. Their organizing meeting included Lucy Stone, Ernestine Rose, Lucretia Mott, and Angelina Grimké Weld, who supported them in passing resolutions advocating full civil and political rights for women as well as blacks when the war ended.

During the next year, they collected over 300,000 signatures, the largest number yet amassed in a single petition campaign. Both Republican politicians and abolitionist activists extended extravagant praise. Members of Congress mailed their petitions under the congressional privilege of franking, or free postage. Charles Sumner, the Massachusetts senator who symbolized radical Republicanism, presented their petitions to the Senate in the spring of 1864. In August, they disbanded the organization. In January 1865, Congress passed the Thirteenth Amendment, abolishing slavery.

The petition campaign enhanced Anthony's and Cady Stanton's importance in antislavery ranks. Their support in 1864 of Wendell Phillips in his successful struggle with William Lloyd Garrison gave them additional leverage. Garrison, always independent and sometimes capricious, called for disbanding the American Anti-Slavery Society on the grounds that the Emancipation Proclamation and congressional resolutions fulfilled antislavery goals. The younger Phillips, second in command to Garrison, disagreed. He trusted neither Congress nor the president to preserve black rights and believed that continued abolitionist pressure was essential. Former Garrisonians, Anthony and Cady Stanton switched allegiance to Phillips, who advocated the continuation of militancy in the postwar period. In the presidential election of 1864, they joined Phillips in an unsuccessful effort to replace Lincoln as Republican party presidential nominee with abolitionist John C. Frémont.

Nevertheless, neither the Republican politicians nor the abolitionist activists ultimately supported woman's rights. The Republican defection came first. In the spring of 1865 Congress began consideration of the Fourteenth Amendment, drafted to guarantee civil and political rights to the freed slaves in the face of continued southern obduracy. But only "males," in the wording of the amendment, were enfranchised. Republican politicians profusely apologized to woman's rights advocates. But, they contended, there was no other way to draft the document. Given the substantial opposition to black suffrage, they argued, the inflammatory issue of woman suffrage had to be kept separate. Congress rejected without consideration woman suffrage petitions and refused to discuss the issue.

The antifeminism of Republican congressmen was clearly revealed in late 1866 when Congress considered a bill to enfranchise black freedmen in the District of Columbia. Again the vote was extended only to male inhabitants. Working through Democratic senators, Cady Stanton and Anthony forced the reluctant upper house to discuss the issue. In the debate, many senators asserted that women were not oppressed and that only a few women bent on notoriety demanded suffrage. Others argued that the corrupt world of politics was no place for intelligent and refined women, who already held substantial power through their respected moral superiority. Furthermore, women's voting would undermine the kind of marriage, sanctioned by God, in which the husband and wife became one and upon which "the whole theory of government and society proceeds." Women's voting would create a divisive independence that would make every home a "hell on earth." Finally, some senators argued that suffrage was a community right, not an individual one, and that the community, through its elected representatives, could restrict suffrage in any manner it chose.

With Congress opposed to woman suffrage, Cady Stanton and Anthony took steps to insure abolitionist support. During the 1866 May Anniversary Week in New York, they transformed the National Woman's Rights Convention, which had not met since 1860, into a new association for the equal rights of both women and blacks. They expected that the American Anti-Slavery Society, meeting concurrently, would merge with their new organization. Their close friend Theodore Tilton, a religious editor and orator of note and the protégé of Henry Ward Beecher, the best-known preacher in the nation, had suggested the merger plan to them. They thought they had secured Wendell Phillips's approval. On the contrary, the abolitionist forces voted against the merger, and Phillips contended that Cady Stanton and Anthony had misunderstood him. Numerous abolitionists as individuals did join the Equal Rights Association. Even Phillips grudgingly extended his personal support, declaring that he thought the Republicans had corrupted the Constitution by introducing the word male into the document. Yet he also enunciated his view that black rights took precedence over woman's. Like the Republicans in Congress, he believed that the issues of black and woman suffrage were each so controversial that linking them would defeat both. "It is the Negro's hour," was the phrase that feminists heard on all sides.

Ignoring such opposition, Cady Stanton and Anthony continued the campaign for votes for women. In 1867 they turned to the New York State Constitutional Convention. But the state legislature dashed their hopes by refusing to recommend to the convention consideration of the issue, despite the many petitions the feminists gathered. Nor did hoped for support materialize from abolitionists who were backing a concurrent bill to enfranchise black males. Moreover, to add insult to injury, a bill licensing prostitution came before the legislature during the 1867 session. The attempt to legalize the sale of sex was infuriating, particularly since the New York bill was only one of a number introduced throughout the nation before city councils and state legislatures. Support for the bill came primarily from a coalition of urban officials and doctors who, influenced by similar British legislation, wanted legal approval to conduct periodic examinations of prostitutes for venereal disease, which had spread alarmingly during the war. In Cady Stanton's view prostitution would be ended when women's wages equaled men's and when women learned self-respect and men learned self-control. Legalization was an insult both to women and to reformers. Anthony and Cady Stanton's lobbying efforts killed the bill in committee.

Cady Stanton's position on the relative merits of black suffrage and woman suffrage never wavered. Like the radical

Republicans and many abolitionists, she viewed the Civil War as much broader than a conflict over slavery. It was a clash of cultures, in which republican ideals had triumphed over southern aristocratic beliefs. Reconstruction offered the opportunity to root out privilege in all forms, to end every aristocracy of class and caste, to bring utopia into being. "This is our opportunity to retrieve the errors of the past," she wrote, "and mould anew the elements of Democracy," to "build a true republic" through reforming the church, the home, and the government. "Through all the trials of this second revolution shall our nation not rise up, with new virtue and strength, to fulfil her mission in leading all the peoples of the earth to the only solid foundation of government, equal rights to all."

Extending rights to black men and not to women reinforced social inequality by expanding the aristocracy of sex. Black males, mostly poor and uneducated, were a liability to the electorate and a danger to women. "All must see that this claim for [black] *male* suffrage is but another experiment in class legislation, another violation of the republican idea." Furthermore, the legislation denied suffrage not only to white but also to black women, who, prey to sexual assault, had been the most victimized by slavery and who even more than black men deserved compensation for wrongs endured.

Cady Stanton regarded the campaign for black male suffrage as cynical and self-interested. As her anger mounted, her rhetoric became increasingly antimale. "So long as woman labors to second man's endeavors and exalt *his sex* above her own, her virtues pass unquestioned; but when she dares to demand rights and privileges for herself, her motives, manners, dress, personal appearance, character, are subjects for ridicule and detraction."

This perspective explains her heavy-handed action in 1867 against Horace Greeley, the editor of the *New York Tribune,* a member of the New York House of Representatives, and chairman of its committee on elections. Greeley, a close friend, had from time to time employed both Cady Stanton and her husband to write for his paper. His wife, Mary Cheney Greeley, was a leader of the 1867 woman suffrage campaign. He had supported woman's rights from its inception, and his newspaper was unique in its sympathetic reporting of woman's rights activities. In the 1867 legislative debates, however, he supported black male suffrage and opposed the vote for women. Rather than attempting to reason with him, Cady Stanton used her considerable ability at sarcasm to ridicule him by heading the first woman suffrage petition presented to the legislature with the name of his wife, written as Mrs. Horace Greeley, and by revealing in testimony before his committee that he had hired a substitute to fight in his place during the war.

Sensitive and insecure, Greeley reacted strongly. He closed the columns of the *Tribune* to Cady Stanton, and, until her death, any reference in the newspaper to her was to Mrs. Henry B. Stanton. She did not care. One by one the Republicans and abolitionists were deserting the woman's cause, and she was increasingly angry. The stage was set for their first major confrontation in the state of Kansas. This confrontation revolved, more than anything else, around Cady Stanton's and Anthony's alliance with a controversial figure named George Francis Train, and in time involved not only Republicans and abolitionists but also fellow feminists.

In the spring of 1867 the legislature of Kansas passed two amendments—one enfranchising women and the other black men—and presented them to the voters for ratification. It was a moment of triumph and challenge to suffragists. Never before had a state legislature passed a woman suffrage bill, nor had the suffragists yet had to mount a campaign directed solely to male voters. Moreover, Kansas occupied a symbolic place in the nation's recent history as the site in the 1850s of combat between free and slave state settlers, of conflict between freedom and tyranny. Involved with the New York constitutional convention, Cady Stanton and Anthony persuaded Lucy Stone and her husband, Henry Blackwell, to take on the initial work of campaigning in Kansas.

During their campaign, Stone and Blackwell thought the

voters would approve the woman suffrage amendment. The response to their speeches seemed favorable; Republican speakers and newspapers were supporting them. Blackwell and Stone left Kansas in May. Cady Stanton and Anthony arrived in August to continue the campaign. By the time of their arrival, however, the situation had changed. Reassessing the prospects for both amendments, the Republicans decided to oppose woman suffrage to ensure the enfranchising of black males. No longer did the woman suffrage amendment appear secure.

Shocked by the situation, Anthony and Cady Stanton did what they could. They extended their campaign throughout the state, contending with the primitive conditions of frontier Kansas. They endured terrible roads, inedible food, and bedbugs. Finding local efforts to coordinate the campaign ineffective, Anthony set up administrative headquarters in Lawrence, and Cady Stanton remained on the road to speak. Virtually the only eastern reformers in the state, they expected endorsements in the eastern reform and Republican press which had previously shown sympathy for woman's rights. Their expectations, however, proved illusory; until the eve of the election the newspapers were silent. Moreover, Phillips and the others refused to advance them any funds from the sizable legacy which a Boston merchant had left both for abolitionism and woman's rights. The eastern abolitionists, it seemed, had abandoned them. They were outraged.

It is against this background of physical exhaustion and perceived betrayal that their controversial action in accepting aid from George Francis Train must be assessed. Train was an enigma, a millionaire who had made a fortune in worldwide ventures before returning to the United States to launch a career as investor and politician. A sometime radical, he supported Irish independence, monetary inflation and central banking, and woman's rights—this last because perhaps he hoped women might support his presidential aspirations. On his own initiative, he addressed the 1867 New York State Constitutional Convention in favor of woman suffrage. The Kansas woman suffrage organization accepted his offer of aid, hoping that he might appeal to Democratic and Irish voters.

Train's eccentric style and his attitude toward blacks were problems. Eastern reformers could not understand how a man who regularly wore purple gloves and full-dress clothing could appeal to Kansas farmers and frontiersmen. More than that, they were convinced he was a racist. But by the time that letters critical of Train reached Kansas, the two New York suffragists were deeply committed to him. They contended that Train, rather than a liability, was a brilliant speaker who attracted large audiences.

In fact, they liked his style. Handsome and charming, he neither smoked nor drank. Cady Stanton came to think of him as a beloved son who had made good and whose objectionable ways she could reform. Besides, as she pointed out to his critics, many militant prewar abolitionists had been eccentric in dress and behavior. Nor did Cady Stanton consider Train a racist. She contended that publicly as well as privately he always supported black rights. Only with regard to voting did he want restraints. He favored general educational qualifications and opposed extension of the franchise to the illiterate and the irresponsible, whether white or black. By 1867 Cady Stanton herself had taken a similar position. Educational qualifications for voting in her view would enfranchise enlightened women, who were the key to reform, and would eliminate from the electorate lower-class, uneducated males, antifeminist and prone to violence.

Behind the conflict over Train also lay his Democratic politics. The Republicanism of most abolitionists, particularly of Henry Blackwell, was more than party allegiance. To them the party was the vehicle of emancipation, union, and justice. Cady Stanton had no such allegiance. The Republicans had attacked her husband. In the Congress, they had refused to accept her woman suffrage petitions, which the Democrats had presented. A believer in laissez faire, she did not like Republican protectionist economic policies, and she accused them of aiding the wealthy at the expense of the masses, of establishing

—in one of her favorite epithets—a new "aristocracy." In 1866 she ran for Congress as an Independent; by 1868 she damned both parties for their antifeminism and elitism and called for a new reform party.

Moreover, Anthony and Cady Stanton liked Train's ideas about reform. Cady Stanton had long been a supporter of free trade and Irish independence; and Train desired to found a new national reform party which would address the issues of sex and class. Train's support of the inflationary proposals of the Greenback party designed to aid farmers and workers also fit well with her antibusiness sentiments. As the Kansas campaign neared its end, Train offered to give Anthony and Cady Stanton what had long seemed beyond the realm of possibility: their own journal. In the face of the hostility of the regular reform press, their previous inability to find backers, and their desire to have a forum for their ideas, they could hardly refuse his offer. And, when the Kansas amendment was defeated, Train financed a speaking tour of major cities on their way back to New York. What might have been an ignominious trip home turned into a triumphant journey. Unfortunately, the mercurial Train found it impossible to remain committed to anything for long, but they had not yet discerned this flaw.

In accepting Train's aid, Cady Stanton and Anthony burned their bridges behind them. Incensed at Republicans and abolitionists, annoyed at Blackwell and Stone, they decided to look in other directions for allies. Since 1863 and the founding of the Woman's Loyal National League, Stanton and Anthony had acted boldly in pursuit of their goals, trying always to keep the good faith of antislavery allies. Now they would experiment with a variety of approaches. In the process they paid little heed to the criticisms of former allies. "It seems to me it would be right and wise to accept aid from the devil himself," wrote Cady Stanton. Her attitude was not really Machiavellian; she was simply very angry at the desertion of former friends and was ready to find new and vigorous supporters on whose loyalty she could count.

After their return to New York from Kansas, Anthony and Cady Stanton plunged into preparations for their new journal. Characteristically, Anthony became the business manager, responsible for finances and administration, and Cady Stanton became coeditor with Parker Pillsbury, a veteran abolitionist who had resigned his position as an antislavery editor in protest over abolitionist opposition to woman suffrage. They named their journal *The Revolution,* a title which broadcast their new independent stance and echoed Cady Stanton's designation of Reconstruction as a second American revolution. "I know we have shocked our old friends," wrote Cady Stanton, "but time will show that Miss Anthony and I are neither idiots nor lunatics." In addition, they enunciated a radical program. No longer did Cady Stanton keep quiet on the issues of divorce and marriage which were increasingly at the core of her feminist philosophy. She consistently attacked the Fourteenth and Fifteenth Amendments for failing to extend voting rights to women. The journal detailed legal and professional discrimination against women and did not hesitate to publicize rape, infanticide, prostitution, and wife-beating, even though mention of these subjects was anathema to respectable Americans. Stanton and Anthony kept the price of the journal low, so that working women could afford it, and they refused to accept patent medicine advertising in contrast to the many editors who relied heavily for revenues on the nation's largest group of advertisers. But as *The Revolution* pointed out, many patent medicines were either worthless or thinly disguised abortifacients or laced with alcohol or laudanum.

Moreover, the journal became a vehicle for affecting new woman's rights strategies. Local woman suffrage associations were everywhere coming into being. These independent groups were composed of remnants of the old organizations and of benevolent women whose public involvement during wartime had sensitized them to discrimination, of professional women benefiting from wartime opportunities and their own determination, and of those incensed by the behavior of the male electorate and their elected representatives. Cady Stanton and Anthony themselves had called the New York group into existence at the time of the 1867 Constitutional Convention, and had worked with local groups in the Kansas campaign. In July 1868 they founded a Woman's Suffrage Association of America to function as a central committee of correspondence for the local organizations.

In addition to their attempts to reestablish and expand the old woman's rights network, they also sought in 1868 to find a new base of support among working women. Woman's rights conventions had periodically addressed the plight of these laborers since the early Seneca Falls days but had made little effort to recruit them as members. Yet Anthony had had an interest in the welfare of factory women since childhood, when her father had operated one of the nation's earliest mills to employ only women workers. Despite advances during the Civil War, in every industry and trade women workers were either relegated to menial positions or paid less than men in the same positions. Women's glove factories which employed many women were appearing in Johnstown; in New York City alone there were 30,000 working women. Cady Stanton could hardly ignore their plight—or their potential power.

In 1868 Cady Stanton and Anthony founded the Workingwoman's Association, aided by several militant tradeswomen attracted by *The Revolution*'s prolabor stance. Their plans for the organization were large: they hoped to establish unions in every industry employing women, to effect the alliance of women of all classes which Cady Stanton expected to be a step toward utopia, and to use the association as a vehicle for a comprehensive reform party. As a way of bringing the classes together, Anthony recruited well-to-do women as members, and Cady Stanton tried, unsuccessfully however, to persuade the organization to adopt woman suffrage, attractive to middle-class women, as a major goal. Concurrently, *The Revolution* proposed the formation of a new People's party devoted to the rights of women, blacks, and laborers. Even before the Kansas campaign, Cady Stanton had suggested such a coalition, and her interest grew in proportion to her disaffection with the existing parties and with her recognition of labor's increased strength marked by the formation in 1866 of the National Labor Union.

However, the high hopes which launched the Working-woman's Association were soon confounded. Although the National Labor Union had initially seemed receptive to the organization and had appointed Anthony chairwoman of a committee on women, within a year the male dominated union severed connections, charging that Anthony had advised women to take jobs away from men. Moreover, women proved exceedingly difficult to organize, characteristically deferential to male supervisors and employers and consistently demoralized by the seasonal nature of their work. Nor did woman suffrage or long-range plans interest them; they sought shorter hours, higher wages, and recognition from the regular unions. Courted by the unions, the working women left the association to join the male dominated unions, and professional and well-to-do members found a more compatible place in Sorosis, a middle-of-the-road group founded in 1868. The Workingwoman's Association ceased to exist.

Serious financial problems also undermined efforts at unionization. By 1869 the inconstant Train, who had journeyed to England on behalf of Irish independence, canceled his backing of *The Revolution*. Train's withdrawal proved disastrous. Despite all their efforts, the two feminists were forced to sell the journal in the spring of 1870.

In its editors' estimation, *The Revolution* had not had time to prove itself. Anthony, in particular, believed that a few more years of financial aid would have made the journal self-sufficient. Yet circulation had reached only 3,000. To respectable Americans, the majority of the reading public, *The Revolution*'s stands on marriage and divorce, on political parties and the economy, were incomprehensible, even immoral. The publication had little impact outside those feminists and radicals who shared its views.

The failure of the Workingwoman's Association and *The Revolution* ended Anthony's and Cady Stanton's united efforts to form organizations that would unite women across class lines. The dream of a political union of the dispossessed—women, blacks, the working classes—continued to haunt Cady Stanton. To Anthony, however, the failure taught one lesson: the woman's movement must not scatter its strength but rather focus on one reform at a time. The reform she chose was suffrage. She now asserted that she had discerned this truth as early as the bloomer agitation, which had been a diversionary action that they should not have repeated. She implied that in divorce reform, in the alliance with Train, and even in worker politics, she had followed Cady Stanton's lead. Anthony now asserted her own authority. In the years ahead she would periodically support Cady Stanton's causes, but her primary devotion was to woman suffrage. Emblematic of her independent course, by 1869 Anthony no longer boarded with Cady Stanton but established permanent residence separately, in Washington, D.C.

At some point in the year during which they founded *The Revolution,* the Workingwoman's Association, and the Woman's Suffrage Association of America, Anthony and Cady Stanton formulated a strategy for their suffrage work for the next thirty years. First, they petitioned both presidential nominating conventions in the summer of 1868 to include woman suffrage planks in their platforms. Both declined, although the Democrats in federal and state legislatures continued to lend aid. Second, they pressed for a separate woman's suffrage amendment rather than for the inclusion of women in the Fifteenth Amendment, then before Congress. Allies in Congress introduced their Sixteenth Amendment—woman suffrage—in March 1869. Third, they transferred their lobbying campaign, focused before this point on the New York State legislature, to Washington, D.C., and the Congress. Borrowing a successful technique from Anthony's prewar Albany campaigns, they began to hold a woman's rights convention in January each year during the congressional session.

In taking these decisive actions, Anthony and Cady Stanton imperiled the unity of the woman's rights movement. Lucy

Stone and Henry Blackwell had been incensed since their support of George Francis Train, their launching of *The Revolution,* and their open radicalism. Stone and her husband had moved to Boston in 1869 to assert leadership over the more conservative and proabolitionist feminist movement there. For several months after the 1869 Washington convention, which Stone and Blackwell did not attend, Anthony and Cady Stanton traveled through the Midwest, making contact with leaders of the new state suffrage societies who by and large had had little identification with antislavery politics. The stage was set for their reassertion of leadership over the movement and also for its division.

The momentum of their involvement with the Workingwoman's Association carried Anthony and Cady Stanton to one further crusade on behalf of workers' concerns. In December 1868 they took up the cause of Hester Vaughan, a young Philadelphian who had been tried, convicted, and sentenced to death for the murder of her illegitimate child. Vaughan had come to Philadelphia from England to be married, only to find that her fiancé was already married. She had secured employment as a domestic. Her employer had seduced her and then fired her on discovering she was pregnant. She could not find another job. When discovered with her dead infant, she was not only close to starvation but was also suffering from puerperal fever, then a common and often fatal postdelivery infection. Despite these complications, an all-male jury judged her guilty of homicide. On sentencing her to death, the judge remarked that infanticide was so common that "some woman must be made an example of."

To Anthony and Cady Stanton, the case was a perfect example of male perfidy. Not only did they publicize it in *The Revolution* but they also held a public protest meeting in New York City against the verdict, ignoring the social convention that no respectable woman ought to be cognizant of such matters. Moreover, Cady Stanton and Elizabeth Smith Miller, acting as her relative's lieutenant, presented a petition on Vaughan's behalf to the governor of Pennsylvania. He eventually pardoned Vaughan on the grounds that there was no evidence that she in fact had taken the child's life.

Cady Stanton's involvement with the Hester Vaughan case was significant to her developing woman's rights strategy. For some time women's sexuality and the proper conception of children had been a primary intellectual concern. *The Revolution* had published reports of thousands of newborn infants abandoned every year on doorsteps and in alleys in New York City. It had also castigated the many thinly disguised abortionists' offices in New York City and the many easily available abortifacients. Cady Stanton condemned both infanticide and abortion; in 1871 she categorized them as disgusting and degrading crimes.

Yet she did not condemn women for resorting to such practices. The problem lay in man's inability to control his desires and in woman's inability to resist. Hester Vaughan and millions of women like her lacked self-discipline and, above all, self-reliance. At a time when suffrage, a political reform, was becoming increasingly important to Anthony, Cady Stanton was drawn to the psychological problem of how to inspire self-reliance in women. Urban crime and violence had deepened her feminism. By 1869, angry against the city and against abolitionist males who refused to support woman suffrage, she asserted that all women were held in slavery by their constant fear of rape. She recommended that every woman buy an immense Newfoundland dog for protection and carry a gun and learn to use it. Asked by dress reform groups once again to endorse the bloomer costume, she refused, replying that women, for safety, ought to adopt male attire and wear suits, coats, and trousers.

Meanwhile, the increasing incidence of abortion and infanticide, as well as venereal disease and prostitution, commanded the concern of other reformers. Conservatives such as Anthony Comstock sought to control these problems by censoring all sources of sexual provocation, including frank discussions of human physiology. Feminists and women reformers more generally looked to the attitudes of men and to the moral education of children as the key to solving the problem. Societies for the promotion of moral education and ad hoc groups to oppose recurrent attempts to legalize prostitution appeared in many areas. The increasing numbers of women doctors and health reformers also addressed these social and sexual issues. Some of them shared Cady Stanton's eugenic views about the role of conception and gestation in human development; most thought that men's inability to control their sexuality was the underlying problem. These disparate individuals and groups later coalesced into the "social purity" movement. They offered significant support for Cady Stanton's views about sexual matters, views that more and more became central to her feminist activism.

Feminism and Evangelism
1869–1880

IN THE SPRING of 1868, several months after the founding of *The Revolution,* Cady Stanton and her family moved to Tenafly, New Jersey, a suburb of New York located in a region of truck farms and summer estates of wealthy New Yorkers, an hour from the city by train. Of all Cady Stanton's homes, the Tenafly house still stands, its basic Victorian design intact. Large and imposing, it is situated in what then were recently developed hills a mile from the Tenafly station. Its exterior is dominated by a columned porch, reminiscent of southern plantation houses and the Livingston mansions on the Hudson. A local architect had designed the house, which was well suited for her large family and for entertaining. Although she made few friends in the local community, whose residents disliked her radicalism, visiting reformers and friends from New York and other New Jersey communities were often there. Above all, the house was a symbol of her independence and her achievement as a self-made, successful woman.

According to Cady Stanton, she bought the house because of soaring property taxes in New York City, because of her children's need for an environment free from urban violence and closer to nature, and especially because of her own desire to retire. But in 1868 she was only fifty-three and quite energetic. Menopause, disorienting to many women, had not troubled her. Current medical theory held that this climacteric, like menstruation and childbearing, drained a woman's energy and exhausted her. Cady Stanton's experience was the opposite. She found release from the burden of childbearing invigorating.

More than that, it seemed to spur her interest in her career. Her reform work during the Civil War and Reconstruction had been centered mostly in New York City. Now she wanted justification for operating in a wider area. Her reaction to menopause gave her one. She felt less involved with her family, less guilty about leaving them. Borrowing from phrenology and the current medical theory that human energy was limited, she argued that her "vital forces," formerly directed to her "reproductive organs," now were "flowing" to her brain. The social impulse was taking precedence over the maternal instinct or, as she put it, "philanthropy" was becoming more important to her than "family sentiment."

In October 1869, she undertook a midwestern lecture tour before a number of lyceums, town forums founded since the 1820s to bring prominent speakers before local audiences. By the 1870s numerous population centers of diverse sizes had lyceums. Reformers were popular speakers before these important institutions of education and entertainment, founded in response both to Americans' appreciation of oratory and their desire for self-improvement through public education. Ralph Waldo Emerson's fame was partly a result of the months he spent on the road, addressing lyceum meetings. Wendell Phillips and William Lloyd Garrison both found guaranteed, responsive audiences at local lyceums. By the late 1860s, as a result of women's visibility in new public roles during the war as nurses, as the organizers and executives of national associations like the Sanitary Commission and the Woman's Loyal National League, and as employees in the work force, the public had become curious about the woman's rights movement.

A New York lyceum booking agency arranged Cady Stanton's tour. Newspaper reporters and local organizers were sufficiently enthusiastic so that in succeeding years she repeated the venture, centering her efforts in New England and the Midwest. Ultimately she became one of the most popular speakers on the lyceum circuit. Most years she spent eight months, from October to June, on the road. She renewed the lecture commitments until 1880, when she was sixty-five.

There were many motivations for her lyceum tours. Personal relationships, ideological commitments, her own emotional makeup—all were involved. Her major public justification was that she needed the fees for family support and for her children's college tuitions. After Henry Stanton's resignation from the Customs House, his income from newspaper reporting and occasional legal work was low. His future as a wage earner, at age sixty-five in 1870, was problematic. Yet Cady Stanton in 1859 had inherited $50,000, a handsome sum, from her father. By 1870 her three eldest sons had finished their educations, and her sister Harriet paid much of the Vassar expenses of her two daughters. Finances, however, were as much rationalization as reason for the lecture tours.

Cady Stanton's lyceum work was a final step in her declaration of independence from her husband and from the strictures about woman's role that she had learned in her childhood. Finally she had freed herself from all social conventions about the proper behavior of a wife and mother. She left Henry Stanton at home with a housekeeper and the four younger children, who ranged between ten and eighteen years. Even the decision to settle in Tenafly was part of her assumption of independence. Every move in their marriage— to Boston, to Seneca Falls, to New York City—had been motivated by Stanton's career commitments. The move to Tenafly was Cady Stanton's choice.

Her declaration of independence from her husband was paralleled by her need to retreat from the New York reform community. Given her dislike of personal confrontation, the heated disagreements of the previous decade had become unbearable. On at least one occasion, in the informal setting of *The Revolution* offices, she had mystified Anthony by agreeing with reformers Theodore Tilton and Henry Ward Beecher that black rights ought to take precedence over woman's rights. Anthony was mortified, but she was not unused to her friend's characteristic desire to please. Moreover, from Cady Stanton's perspective, their vigorous actions of the previous decade had met only with unfair criticism, even from Lucy Stone and her supporters. The circle of disagreement widened and, ultimately including even Susan Anthony, further impelled Cady Stanton toward independence.

The final confrontation between abolitionists and woman's rights advocates took place in May 1869 at the annual meeting in New York City of the Equal Rights Association, the organization that Anthony and Cady Stanton had founded in 1864 as a means of joining the two groups. For some time the organization had been little more than a debating forum, but no one involved was yet ready to disband it and to reveal publicly the fragile comity of the seemingly united reform community. The 1869 proceedings were more boisterous than ever, the debates over the two reforms more embittered. When Anthony and Cady Stanton criticized the Fifteenth Amendment, they were booed and accused of being racist. A resolution was introduced demanding that the two women withdraw from the organization.

The appearance of a number of free love advocates created even more excitement. In line with their egalitarian goals, woman's rights supporters had always extended their podiums to reformers of all kinds. The free love forces advocated a variety of social and sexual communal arrangements. Many of them, like those at the famous Oneida Community, did little to publicize their views. Others were vocal and often appeared at woman's rights conventions, contributing to the turmoil of the 1869 Equal Rights Association meeting. Many reformers suspected that Cady Stanton, who chaired the meeting, was an advocate of free love because of her libertarian views on divorce and birth control.

Throughout the meeting, Cady Stanton and Anthony felt increasingly powerless. The delegates defeated the resolution demanding their withdrawal but voted in favor of another objectionable proposal, introduced by Frederick Douglass, which pledged support for the Fifteenth Amendment. Lucy Stone and Henry Blackwell tried to effect a compromise, but the polarization of positions had gone too far. Upon the adjournment of the convention, Cady Stanton and Anthony took matters into their own hands. Without further ado, they called into being a National Woman Suffrage Association. Its goal was a sixteenth amendment for woman suffrage.

Although they tried to make the organization appear to be a spontaneous expression of majority sentiment, it was effected hastily and with little publicity. None of Anthony's and Cady Stanton's antagonists were present, and the 100 participants were all women. The majority of delegates were from New York (fifty-three) and the west (twenty), where Anthony and Cady Stanton had gained a following during the speaking tour of the previous months. They had doubtless considered founding the organization for some time.

The final division in the woman's movement was probably inevitable. In November, 1869, one month after Cady Stanton had begun her lyceum tours, Stone and Blackwell organized a rival American Woman Suffrage Association in Cleveland— the location an obvious play for western support. The Boston leaders themselves were incensed. Now fifty-one years old, Lucy Stone had become both more conservative and more powerful. Retired from the woman's movement for some time, she did not appreciate the extent to which Anthony had come to dominate it and, along with Cady Stanton, to regard it as her own creation. Personality as well as politics lay behind the division in feminist ranks. Most of the other prewar leaders— Martha Wright, Ernestine Rose, Lucretia Mott—were content to remain Anthony's lieutenants; Antoinette Brown Blackwell, Lucy Stone's sister-in-law, had had seven children and remained for the most part retired from reform. Stone's husband, Henry Blackwell, had become a successful businessman whose money was available for feminist purposes. Powerful in his own right, he was as much a copartner in reform with Stone as was Anthony with Cady Stanton.

Stone and Blackwell were loyal abolitionists and Republicans. Legal and political discrimination troubled them more than woman's social burdens. They regarded Cady Stanton's zealous crusade as romantic and counterproductive, and objected to her focus on marriage and divorce. Above all, they wanted to have nothing to do with the free love label often applied to her.

Cady Stanton consistently advocated state sanctioned marriage, but she refused to declare publicly that the free love advocates were wrong. Indeed, she sympathized with their efforts to achieve woman's sexual liberation and saw their agitation as a healthy attempt to bring the issues of marriage and divorce to public attention. When Elizabeth Smith Miller, confused by her relative's stance on free love, asked Cady Stanton directly if she espoused the ideology, she replied that she was opposed to the sexual promiscuity of many of the free lovers and advocated monogamy because, referring to her hereditarian beliefs, "everything short of this makes mongrel, sensual progeny." But, Cady Stanton continued, she could be counted a believer in free love if by the term Smith Miller meant "woman's right to give her body to the man she loves and no other, to become a mother or not as her desire, judgment, and conscience may dictate . . . , to be absolute sovereign of herself."

Cady Stanton often attacked the critics of free love, particularly those opponents who denounced anyone who raised a sexual issue as a free lover. Her libertarian position had solid grounding. Since the days of the Seneca Falls convention and the bloomer agitation, reactionaries had identified the woman's rights movement with extremists and had inflated the influence of free love out of all proportion to its real power. Cady Stanton dismissed the free love charges as a tactic that reactionaries used when they thought themselves threatened. She pointed out that religious liberals had once been called infidels and feminists strong-minded. The epithets were meaningless. "Each age has some word of momentous import," she wrote, "with which to hound the lovers of truth and progress."

Such views did not calm the inflamed tempers of conservative feminists, already annoyed by Anthony and Cady Stanton's criticism of abolitionists, their acceptance of Democratic aid, and their independent actions. Suffragist Olympia Brown remembered that in 1869 the country was in the midst of a free love panic. "One could hardly speak in the most academic or speculative way of the marriage or divorce question without being accused of free love bias." Not only did Cady Stanton regularly take up the divorce issue but she even aired the topic of sex in speaking about seduction and infanticide in the well-publicized Hester Vaughan case.

All those involved in the events of 1869 compared the break to the 1839 abolitionist division between the militant Garrisonians and the New York moderates. In retrospect, however, the actual differences between the two feminist organizations were not substantial. Claiming that the New Yorkers controlled the National Woman Suffrage Association (NWSA) by weight of numbers, the American Woman Suffrage Association (AWSA) chose delegates to its policymaking conventions through equal state representation. The AWSA centered its efforts on state legislatures rather than the federal government—partly because the NWSA had gotten to Washington first. Both organizations focused on suffrage, and Anthony soon played down her social radicalism. The schism, however, engendered bitter personal animosities that did not abate for a full generation. For twenty-one years, until reuniting in 1890, the two organizations remained separate.

Cady Stanton did not respond with equanimity to the division. Detesting violent arguments with former friends, she publicly maintained a philosophical stance. Privately, however, she seethed at the vituperation directed against Anthony and herself, "the ridicule, persecution, denunciation, detraction, the unmixed bitterness of our cup for the past two years, when even friends crucified us." After the 1869 Equal Rights Association meeting and the formation of the NWSA, she avoided woman suffrage conventions. In the years ahead, Anthony often had to come to her home and, by means of argument and blandishment, cajole her into attending.

Moreover, her relationship with Anthony also encountered difficulties. The problems were both personal and ideological. Although the two never openly quarreled, Cady Stanton often felt crowded by Anthony's increasing personal dominance and her incessant work demands. After 1869 Anthony did not hesitate to pressure her friend for support. Publicly they rarely disagreed, but privately they criticized one another, particularly after Anthony had adopted suffrage as her main goal, in contrast with Cady Stanton's social utopianism. As early as 1865, Cady Stanton had written to Anthony that she was not willing to be bullied when they disagreed. In 1870 she wrote to Martha Wright that she would no longer allow Anthony to force her into anything. In 1871 she characterized their friendship as perfect—so long as they were "equals . . . neither assuming to control the other." She did not aid Anthony in repaying the $10,000 debt which *The Revolution* had accumulated before its sale to new ownership in 1870, even though Anthony devoted most of her lecture and publication fees for the next five years to retiring the obligation. In a rather cavalier manner indicative of her disaffection, Cady Stanton counseled Anthony to give up feminist activism for a time, to forget about *The Revolution*'s debt, and to amass some personal savings. She wrote Anthony's sister that the Anthony family should pay off the debt, even though, as Anthony wrote in her diary, "they got none of the good from *The Revolution* and Mrs. Stanton got a great deal."

The rift between Anthony and Cady Stanton deepened with the latter's growing sense of isolation within the organized movement. Many of the new, younger leaders within the NWSA, who had emerged to prominence after the Civil War, shared Anthony's commitment to suffrage and looked on social reform as secondary. Well educated, their feminism was more the outgrowth of their desire for increased personal opportunity than of a sense of woman's subordination. They had profited from the proliferation of women's roles during

the war; increasingly colleges and the professions were open
to them. They had not experienced the discrimination that
Cady Stanton's generation had met; they did not demonstrate,
as she put it, "the underlying devotion and self-sacrifice that
those of us feel who have given up to it [the woman's move-
ment] the heyday of their lives, sentiments, and actions."
Without children of her own and agreeing with their emphasis
on suffrage, Anthony increasingly forged a rapport with the
younger women which Cady Stanton did not share. The
breech in the old friendship widened.

Cady Stanton's concern over the conservatism of these new,
younger associates was heightened in the spring of 1870 when
many supported the efforts of Theodore Tilton and Henry
Ward Beecher to reconcile the NWSA and the AWSA. In 1869
the AWSA elected Henry Ward Beecher its first president, and
the next spring Tilton created a Union Suffrage Association
with himself as president. Over Cady Stanton's objections he
persuaded NWSA members to merge their organization with
his in the hopes of an eventual merger with the AWSA. In the
end, however, Stone and Blackwell refused amalgamation, and
the plan failed. Anthony reconstituted the NWSA with Cady
Stanton as president. But Cady Stanton was angered by
Beecher's and Tilton's actions and by NWSA members who
had supported them. "It seems to me most humiliating," she
wrote, "that both of our associations have men as presidents."
Her resolve to continue on an independent course increased.

Anthony and Cady Stanton attempted to resolve their differences in a joint tour of the Pacific coast in 1871. They stopped
on the way for speaking engagements, sometimes on im-
promptu summonses from groups of women who, knowing
their itinerary, came to local train stations to hear them. Their
most memorable planned engagement was in Salt Lake City,
Utah, capital of the Mormon territory. The secession of several
hundred Mormons who opposed polygamy, a recent Supreme
Court decision that a man's first wife and her children were his
only legal heirs, and the granting of woman suffrage by the
territorial legislature in order to stop federal incursions on the

Mormon polity had created an uncharacteristically sympathetic climate in Utah to the woman's rights message.

To their surprise, the response to their speeches was enthusiastic: Mormon women remained in the tabernacle for five hours to hear them speak and discuss woman's issues. They were impressed by the sense of order and mission in the community, and Cady Stanton was even swayed by Mormon arguments for polygamy, especially for the "sacredness of motherhood," meaning abstinence from sexual relations, during pregnancy and lactation. Then and later Cady Stanton often argued that polygamy was in fact no worse than the man-made marriages of the regular society.

But the rest of the tour was a mixed success. San Francisco newspapers gave extravagant praise to Cady Stanton's interviews and speeches but were harshly critical of Anthony. According to the *San Francisco Chronicle,* "Miss Anthony is by no means as successful a lecturer as Mrs. Stanton. Whilst the one is gifted with wonderful oratorical powers. . . the other is hesitating and halty in her style." Cady Stanton's lectures on maternity and even on her brand of free love brought only compliments, but Anthony was excoriated for mentioning that men bore responsibility for the crime of San Franciscan Laura Fair, a high-class prostitute who had killed her prominent lover and was currently in prison, awaiting trial.

The two vacationed together in Yosemite, but the San Francisco experience embittered Anthony, particularly because she felt that Cady Stanton had not given her sufficient public support. She was not unhappy when her friend returned east, leaving Anthony to finish the rest of the tour. "There is no alternative," wrote Anthony, "whoever goes into a parlor or before an audience with that woman does it at the price of a fearful overshadowing" because of the "brilliant scintillations" from her "never-exhausted magazine." Although they occasionally jointly toured the Midwest for suffrage and woman's rights in the years ahead, the California venture of 1871 was their last major mutual commitment for some time. In later years both feminist leaders would agree that the best period in their relationship had been during the Kansas campaign and the first months of *The Revolution,* before any significant difference of opinion had emerged.

Cady Stanton could not sustain indefinitely the momentum from her anger of the 1860s. Detesting personal controversy as she did, the lyceum tours in the West were a way of escape. Yet more than psychological retreat motivated her tours. Since the founding of the woman's movement, Cady Stanton had seen her role as that of its radical conscience, challenging complacency and raising controversial issues. In the 1870s she feared that the demand for the ballot might swallow up any comprehensive reform program. She had introduced suffrage in 1848, when the proposal had been new and shocking. Now, accepted by all feminists and actually in force in the territories of Wyoming and Utah, its agitation had become predictable to some, tiresome to others. To retain her leadership and rally the movement behind a comprehensive program, she assumed an independent stance.

She chose a public forum to give weight to her ideas. This time the forum was not a woman's rights gathering, in contrast with those of Seneca Falls in 1848 and New York City in 1860. Rather she and Anthony called a public meeting in the spring of 1870 to protest the judicial decision in the well publicized McFarland-Richardson trial. Like the Hester Vaughan case two years before, this trial involved the issues of women's legal rights and their treatment by men. Albert McFarland, a sometime New York City lawyer, was charged with the murder of James Richardson, a *Tribune* reporter who had become involved with McFarland's wife, Abby Sage. The details of the case were dramatic and controversial. The prosecution contended that McFarland was an alcoholic, unable to hold a job, who periodically beat his wife. In order to support the family she took up acting and dramatic reading and moved them into a boarding house, where she met Richardson. Finally, unable to stand McFarland's abuse, she secured a divorce in Indiana and intended to marry Richardson when the murder occurred.

The defense contended that McFarland was not an alcoholic and that Sage was a loose woman whose affair with Richardson prompted her divorce action.

The murder itself took place in the *Tribune* office. Richardson lived for a number of hours after the attack, and he and Sage were married in the *Tribune* office, with Henry Ward Beecher officiating. McFarland's lawyer, flamboyant and known for spectacular defenses, persuaded the judge to rule that the Indiana divorce was invalid, that Sage was still McFarland's wife, and that she could not testify against her husband, even though she was the major witness to his alcoholism and violence. To all intents and purposes the all-male jury acquitted McFarland by ruling him guilty by reason of temporary insanity—a verdict which implied that legitimate anger had prompted the murder. McFarland was released and given custody of the couple's child.

For weeks the McFarland-Richardson trial was front page news. It had a significant impact on Cady Stanton, who had just completed her first lyceum tour and been forced to resign the NWSA presidency to Theodore Tilton. The parallels to the Hester Vaughan case were striking, especially after the *Tribune* published Sage's tragic account of her marriage—an account which the court had not allowed her to present at the trial. As they had in the Vaughan case, Cady Stanton and Anthony arranged a public protest meeting from which men were excluded. The 2,000 women who attended constituted the largest such audience ever assembled in New York City.

Cady Stanton's remarks were impassioned. She called the verdict the Dred Scott decision of the woman's movement, comparing it to the Supreme Court's prewar vindication of black slavery. It will bring, she declared, a new phase to woman's rights. "As personal liberty, in the true order, comes before political freedom, woman must first be emancipated from the old bondage of a divinely ordained allegiance to man before her pride of sex can be so roused as to demand the rights of citizenship." In this new struggle, she promised, "as I had hitherto devoted my life to the enfranchisement of women, so my future days should be spent in teaching woman her duties to herself." Her new role was to include "the physical and intellectual education of women for wifehood and maternity, and the alteration and modification of our divorce laws."

Involvement with the McFarland-Richardson trial gave Cady Stanton the final justification for continuing her lyceum tours and recasting her reform message around personal and social relations. Her purpose was moral and missionary. She now put into practice her old Garrisonian convictions about the need to change a nation's consciousness through proselytizing. She liked to preach and pray, to be a pundit and prophet. Oratory and persuasion appealed to her romantic nature and echoed from the environment of her youth. Evangelical lecturing relieved her of administrative detail and organizational fetters. She may have recalled her beloved father's tales of his early days as a lawyer, when he had ridden circuit in the near wilderness of upstate New York. Many of her friends and fellow feminists also traveled the lyceum trail, and she encountered them in train stations and in hotel lobbies as she passed from town to town. She saw herself as part of a band of agitators spreading a gospel of feminism and reform.

The work was not easy. The traveling was arduous, and the schedules exhausting. "It was often necessary to travel night and day," she wrote, "sometimes changing cars at midnight, and perhaps arriving at the destination half an hour or less before going on the platform, and starting again on the journey upon leaving it." She traveled "in a constant fever of anxiety" that she would miss her train or encounter accidents, floods, or blizzards. Once when touring northern Iowa, she found that all the roads were snowbound. She hired a sleigh and driver and made the circuit by traveling over fields and prairies atop the snow. In Nebraska in 1872 the only means of conveyance were hazardous open wagons. When one overturned, badly hurting several passengers, the accident left Cady Stanton for days with an aching back and head. Sleeping accommodations were often crude. During the Nebraska tour she had to sleep on a broken couch in a hotel lobby because all the rooms had been taken by spectators at a local murder trial.

However, there were compensations. She enjoyed testing her stamina. "Everybody regards me with wonder for my endurance and cheerfulness," she wrote her sisters. "I enjoy life under the most adverse circumstances." Her sense of humor sustained her. En route by train from Houston to New York she played whist and discussed woman's rights with a group of sympathetic army officers and dismissed a dyspeptic looking clergyman who lectured her on the evils of cardplaying by parodying social Darwinism to him. Their total disagreement over cardplaying made further discussion pointless; they would have to wait for "the slow process of evolution" to give to each "a higher standard." When her suitcase containing copies of Representative Benjamin Butler's favorable minority report on woman suffrage fell by accident into the Platte River, her first thought was that the mercurial Butler had been in hot water all his life and now his report was perishing in cold water.

Even when traveling she was an outspoken reform advocate. Most women on trains rarely left their seats or engaged in conspicuous behavior. In contrast, Cady Stanton talked to other passengers, walked the aisles for exercise, and got off the train when it stopped. She opened windows for better ventilation and relieved mothers of crying babies, soothing the infants by removing their swaddling bands and bathing them. To many mothers she outlined her own child care regimen and convinced them of the foolishness of using tranquilizing syrups laced with laudanum, and of swaddling their babies—practices which to her surprise seemed still widespread. Based on these experiences, she incorporated child care advice into her popular lecture, "Marriage and Maternity."

By all accounts, few could rival Cady Stanton's stature as a speaker. Hearing her in 1888, when Cady Stanton was seventy-five, Swedish feminist Alexandra Gripenberg described the "unshakable conviction" and the "fire of genius" of her oratory; phrases running through descriptions of her platform effect and indicating the force of her appeal. Learning from the evangelical, antislavery, and political orators of her youth and maturity, she had mastered the florid emotionalism which captivated nineteenth-century audiences. When in command of the podium she was firm and decisive. One observer had studied her "for hours at a sitting," presiding over New York City meetings. "When the brazen [free love] women who have brought such bad fame to the woman's rights movement were trying to secure 'the floor,' and gaunt fanatics of my own sex were contending with them for that 'privilege,' and the mob was hissing or shouting, the tact with which Mrs. Stanton managed that whole assembly was a marvel."

Her impact was as comforting as it was powerful and uplifting. Gripenberg reported that her voice was low, in the alto range, and that it was soothing. Her speeches always contained humorous stories calculated to make her audiences laugh. Most descriptions mention her natural wit; the *San Francisco Chronicle* in 1871 summed up her appearance in one word: jolly. Reporters also noted her graciousness and lack of the masculine manner they criticized in many woman's rights speakers.

Married and the mother of seven children, Cady Stanton became a favorite of the public and the press which, still critical of her aims, usually presented her as a symbol of benevolent maternity. Journalists characteristically compared her to Martha Washington or Queen Victoria, revered female figures of the age. "Plump as a partridge" went one description in 1870, "of warm complexion, with a well-formed head, adorned with white hair, put up unstiffly in puffs, she would anywhere be taken for the mother of a governor or president." "Stately Mrs. Stanton has secured much immunity" wrote popular author Grace Greenwood, "by a comfortable look of motherliness and a sly benignancy in her smiling eyes, even though her arguments have been bayonet thrusts and her words gun shots." Contemporary norms of beauty lent approval to the weight which years of heavy eating and seven pregnancies had added to her naturally bulky frame. Her careful attention to dress and her luxuriant, naturally curly white hair provided a comforting example for older women. Even young girls, by her account, flocked around her everywhere, demanding "a kiss, a curl, an autograph."

In addition to her regular lyceum lectures, generally delivered in the evenings, Cady Stanton spoke before church congregations and reform societies. She often scheduled afternoon lectures on the topic of "enlightened motherhood," in which she presented her eugenic ideas about the proper conception and gestation of children. To teach independence and avoid embarrassment, only women were admitted to these afternoon lectures. But even her evening lectures before mixed audiences often focused on marriage and sexual relations. For these lectures she chose noncontroversial titles like "Home Life" or "Our Girls"—her two favorite lyceum lectures—in an obvious attempt to play down her reputation for radicalism. The content of the lectures, however, drew directly from her feminist ideology. "Home Life," for example, contained rousing pleas for liberalized divorce, equality between men and women, coeducation, the defeat of legislation which sought to license prostitution, and self-control in sexual relations.

Cady Stanton's sexual evangelism roused much criticism within the woman's movement. Longtime coworker Frances Dana Gage of Ohio thought that the emphasis was wrongheaded because of woman's extreme fear of sexuality. Most women, according to Gage, "even in the bedchamber or in the most private conversation start back in alarm, that cannot be controlled, from the immodesty of the thing." In reply, Cady Stanton argued that audiences responded more favorably to her lectures on marriage and divorce than to her speeches on suffrage. The topic of enlightened motherhood, she asserted, spoke directly to the immediate needs of women who saw little personal benefit in the vote. Often, she explained, her lectures to women alone lasted three hours or more "and then they hunger still. The new gospel of fewer children, and a healthy, happy maternity is gladly received."

The *San Francisco Examiner* may have overstated the case when it contended in 1871 that Cady Stanton's visit had sparked a social revolution. But taken together with the propagandizing of others and the increasing number of manuals on sexuality and contraception available, her lectures contributed to an effort on the part of American women to take some control over their sexual and reproductive lives. There was a striking decrease in the number of children American women bore over the course of the nineteenth century; birth control was apparently widespread. Moreover, as a radical representative of the social purity movement, Cady Stanton contributed to the growing reaction against the prohibition of open discussion of sexual matters, laying the groundwork for later reform movements directed toward sexual liberation.

Her lyceum tours significantly influenced the lives of individual women but did not produce committed woman's rights advocates. Women's organizations expanded greatly in size and number during the late nineteenth century, but the moderate, not the radical ones, attracted large numbers. Organizations like the Women's Christian Temperance Union, which dated from 1874, and woman's clubs like New York City's Sorosis benefited from women's postwar willingness to join together in activities outside the home. In keeping with the generally conservative tenor of the times, even Cady Stanton's NWSA became increasingly conservative as the century progressed.

Nevertheless, in 1871 Cady Stanton became involved with Victoria Woodhull, an outspoken radical who demanded sexual and social equality and who was president of the small American wing of Karl Marx's International Workingman's Association. The noted New York feminist first became cognizant of the younger newcomer about the time of the 1870 McFarland-Richardson trial. Woodhull and her sister, Tennessee Claflin, had shattered tradition that spring by establishing the first woman's brokerage firm on Wall Street, an exclusive male bastion of finance and security trading. Soon thereafter,

Woodhull announced her candidacy for the presidency and established her own journal, *Woodhull and Claflin's Weekly,* devoted to radicalism and feminism. In January 1871, she electrified the NWSA Washington convention by arranging through her own congressional connections to speak in favor of woman suffrage before the influential House Committee on the Judiciary, which had not yet extended an invitation to NWSA representatives.

Cady Stanton, who did not attend the 1871 convention, did not meet Woodhull until May of that year. Like many other woman's rights activists, she was suspicious of Woodhull at first. One of ten children of an itinerant peddler father and a spiritualist mother, Woodhull was a product of the Ohio back country and its culture of spiritualism, medicine shows, and theatrical troupes. She was flamboyant with a daring that not even Cady Stanton could match. The funding for her brokerage firm and personal fortune derived from the influence she and her clairvoyant sister exercised over multimillionaire Cornelius Vanderbilt. Scandalous stories regularly circulated about her relationships with men. Shortly after the 1871 Washington convention, Cady Stanton cautioned Anthony against involvement with Woodhull for fear of a repetition of the Train affair. Initially the similarity between Train and Woodhull—both radical, eccentric millionaires—was not lost on Cady Stanton.

But Woodhull's radical ideology did not differ greatly from that of Cady Stanton, who recently had felt isolated from the mainstream woman's movement. Like Cady Stanton, Woodhull traced social injustice to the sexual oppression of women. She, too, was a utopian influenced by phrenologists and physiologists. She also argued that the conditions of conception and gestation profoundly influenced human development. Even though Woodhull had allied herself with the free love movement, had damned marriage, and had asserted woman's right to love whomever she pleased, she favored monogamous relationships. In contrast to Cady Stanton, however, Woodhull stressed woman's need for sexual fulfilment. Where Cady

Stanton took care, in discussing sex, that "the presentation of facts and philosophy [was] quite unobjectionable," Woodhull was explicit and potentially offensive to women of their day.

Woodhull's sympathy for the poor and the workers, her muckraking attacks on American business, and her statements about the need for social revolution found resonance in Cady Stanton's own rhetoric. Moreover, Woodhull was intent on achieving a unified coalition of the left—a goal which remained Cady Stanton's dream even after she had abandoned her own efforts to bring it into being. The announcement of Woodhull's presidential candidacy, her attempts to take over the NWSA, her leadership of Marx's International Workingman's Association—all could be interpreted as part of a plan to effect the very reform party that Cady Stanton had wanted since her disillusionment with Reconstruction politics.

Woodhull had also demonstrated political sensitivity. Her stirring address before the House Committee on the Judiciary won the approval of NWSA leaders, and she brought new energy to the organization by proposing a vigorous plan of action. Refurbishing a current argument which Cady Stanton herself had previously put forth with little effect, Woodhull contended that the Fourteenth Amendment actually enfranchised women under its provision which asserted the rights of citizenship without reference to sex. Thus a campaign for a sixteenth woman suffrage amendment was unnecessary, because women already had the constitutional right to vote. Woodhull called on all activist women to register, to vote, and, if challenged, to take their cases to court to prove the suffragists' constitutional argument. This strategy, known as the "new departure," was especially appreciated by Cady Stanton. "With this view our manner of agitation is radically changed," she wrote. "Instead of forming county societies, rolling up petitions against unjust laws or in favor of further amendments to state and national constitutions, we demand our rights at the ballot box, in the courts, before judiciary committees of congress and in annual Washington conventions."

Cady Stanton's reservations about Woodhull evaporated after their initial meeting during the May 1871 New York convention. Beautiful and eloquent, Woodhull had hypnotic eyes and an unusually free, arresting manner. In rebuttal to the scandalous stories about her new friend, Cady Stanton explained that Woodhull's sexuality and "ability to love"—potentially uplifting qualities which most women denied—had been for Woodhull "the means of a grand development." They were further drawn together by their mutual annoyance at AWSA leaders, meeting concurrently in New York City, who officially condemned Woodhull and free love doctrines. Even Susan Anthony was annoyed by the AWSA action, describing it as a sick attempt to avoid touching "even the hem of the Woodhull garments."

Finally, mutual anger against the Beecher family was an additional bond. Evidence was accumulating that Henry Ward Beecher had seduced Cady Stanton's close friend and occasional coworker, Elizabeth Tilton, the wife of Theodore Tilton. Catherine Beecher and Harriet Beecher Stowe, Henry Ward Beecher's well-known sisters, had taken conservative positions on the woman's issue. In a recent bestselling novel, *My Wife and I,* Harriet Beecher Stowe had parodied both Woodhull and Cady Stanton. Catherine Beecher was loudly critical of Woodhull. Privately Cady Stanton penned a vitriolic portrait of Catherine Beecher as a "narrow, bigoted, arrogant woman," who might have become humane had she ever "loved with sufficient devotion, passion, & abandon any of Adam's sons to have forgotten herself, her God, her *family*, & her propriety, & endured for a brief space of time the world's coldness, ridicule, or scorn." Cady Stanton knew well the powerful role that families played in shaping character and careers. But she had broken with her own and had emerged, like Woodhull, courageous and self-reliant because of her rebellion.

Cady Stanton's identification with Woodhull was strong. She continued to defend her even after Woodhull's tempestuous personal affairs were aired in court in late May as a result of the cruelty suit which her mother, who lived with her, brought against her husband. Indeed, the litigation not only exposed the rift between Woodhull's close relatives but also revealed that her former husband as well as her present spouse resided in her home. Even this extreme violation of Victorian conventions did not shock Cady Stanton, who remained loyal to Woodhull. To friends and opponents, Cady Stanton repeated that Woodhull's private life was her own business and that concern about woman's purity was usually motivated by men's hypocrisy, their desire to turn women against each other, and their fear of strong and famous women who, like Woodhull, Mary Wollstonecraft, or George Sand, lived free personal lives. She compared Woodhull to Hester Prynne in Nathaniel Hawthorne's *Scarlet Letter,* publicly judged by the very man responsible for her sin.

As with Train, the capriciousness of Woodhull's character was not immediately apparent. And Cady Stanton was often away from New York and occupied with other concerns. In the summer of 1871 she went to California with Anthony. In the fall her mother died. Lyceum tours occupied the winter and spring of 1872. Meanwhile, Woodhull continued to demonstrate loyalty to woman suffrage. To implement her "new departure" policy she voted in New York City, along with a number of women nationwide.

In the spring of 1872 a schism in the Republican party resulted in a Liberal-Republican presidential nomination of Horace Greeley, Cady Stanton's one-time friend, and he insultingly refused her offer of aid from woman's rights forces. "I had rather," she wrote, "see Beelzebub president than Greeley." Annoyed and casting about for allies, Cady Stanton seized on an alliance which Victoria Woodhull proposed. With Anthony on tour, Woodhull persuaded Cady Stanton to issue a proclamation pledging NWSA support for Woodhull's newly formed Equal Rights party, the vehicle for her presidential aspirations.

What Cady Stanton saw as a woman's rights opportunity, Anthony viewed as a threatening attempt on the part of Woodhull to take control of the NWSA. She rushed back to New

York City to prevent a merger of the two organizations during the May Anniversary Week meetings. She found, indeed, that many NWSA delegates were committed to Woodhull, and she retained control of the convention only by asserting her authority as the lessee of the meeting hall. (Since the law prohibited married women from making contracts without their husbands' consents, the unmarried Anthony had signed NWSA contracts.) Dictatorially seizing the podium, Anthony refused to allow Woodhull to speak, and imperiously turned out the lights when Woodhull refused to leave.

Anthony's actions so infuriated Cady Stanton that she immediately resigned the NWSA presidency. But she did not support Woodhull's Equal Rights party. Nor was she ever again willingly involved with Woodhull. Available evidence does not reveal exactly what occurred. Perhaps Anthony disclosed additional scandal about Woodhull or threatened to expose their own differences publicly. A face-to-face confrontation in Tenafly the night before the meeting may have been sufficient to trigger Cady Stanton's dislike of offending close friends. In her diary Anthony wrote that she never had been so hurt as by the "folly of Stanton." In any event, the situation posed clear alternatives to Cady Stanton: she could support either Anthony or Woodhull. She chose Anthony.

Within a year Woodhull's career was at its nadir. Her presidential campaign was a fiasco. She was near financial ruin, abandoned by most of her supporters, and forced to give up her journal. She had taken on the nation's political establishment and been rebuffed. In late 1872 she struck back at the nation's moral establishment by revealing the details of what she claimed was a love affair between Henry Ward Beecher and Elizabeth Tilton, both friends of Cady Stanton and involved in woman's rights.

Cady Stanton long remained sympathetic to Woodhull. When Henry Blackwell in private correspondence with Cady Stanton in the summer of 1872 characterized Woodhull's Equal Rights party as a "motley crowd of disreputables and visionaries upon a crusade of egotism," Cady Stanton responded by praising Woodhull's 1870 speech and her new departure policy before the House Judiciary Committee. She confessed that the alliance with Woodhull may have been a blunder, but she argued that at least Woodhull, like Train, had kept public attention on the woman issue, and that her free love radicalism had made woman suffrage by comparison seem moderate and respectable.

Cady Stanton's final public appraisal of her former radical ally in the late 1870s is a statement of lush imagery which may indicate the extent to which—perhaps unconsciously—she wished she could have followed Woodhull in her exploits. "Leaping over the brambles that were too high for us to see over them," wrote Cady Stanton, "she broke a path into their close and thorny interstices, with a steadfast faith that glorious principle would triumph at last over conspicuous ignominy, although her life might be sacrificed." But in the end Woodhull went too far. "And when, with a meteor's dash, she sank into a dismal swamp, we could not lift her out of the mire nor buoy her through the deadly waters."

VII

The Return to Suffrage
1872–1890

DISASSOCIATED FROM Woodhull, no longer president of the NWSA, angry with Anthony, Cady Stanton momentarily considered giving up woman's rights for theological speculation or labor agitation. While floundering, she came across on unexpected opportunity. Only a few weeks after the Woodhull fiasco, Lucy Stone and Henry Blackwell approached her to join them in support of the Republican candidate for president, incumbent Ulysses S. Grant. Cady Stanton was not enthusiastic about Grant, but the Republican platform mentioned woman's rights favorably, Stone and Blackwell outlined exciting plans for a nationwide convention of women to endorse Grant, and Cady Stanton was bitterly opposed to Horace Greeley, the Democratic as well as the Liberal-Republican candidate. In addition, Anthony had decided to support Grant and had secured paid commissions from the Republican party for a number of woman's rights speakers. "Let bygones be bygones," Cady Stanton wrote Lucy Stone. "In union there is strength."

Although their joint work in the Grant campaign brought a reconciliation between Anthony and Cady Stanton, the effort at amalgamation between the AWSA and the NWSA proved abortive. Cady Stanton accepted one of Anthony's commissions and stumped for Grant in several northern states, but there was little joint activity between the two suffrage organizations. Within a few years, the occasional correspondence between Boston and Washington was icy in tone. Stone refused in no uncertain terms to sign the NWSA Declaration of Woman's Rights, formulated to mark the nation's centennial in 1876; she would have nothing to do with Anthony's and Cady Stanton's history of the woman suffrage movement.

Despite Cady Stanton's rapprochement with Anthony, she was not entirely enthusiastic about her friend's woman's rights strategy during the post-Woodhull years. In order to reinvigorate the new departure policy and to end any identification of the NWSA with Woodhull, Anthony registered and voted in the 1872 elections. As she anticipated, she was prosecuted, brought to trial, judged guilty, and fined in what became a celebrated incident of the nineteenth-century woman's movement.

Cady Stanton's only gesture of support was to write several articles explaining Anthony's constitutional argument. Challenged by a mutual friend to justify her lukewarm efforts, Cady Stanton's feeble defense was that she was so enraged against all men—"the whole dynasty of tyrants"—that she did not have "one stagnant drop of blood in my veins for any single act of insult." Perhaps Anthony, always more indignant about Blackwell's and Stone's behavior, had annoyed Cady Stanton by opposing the 1872 union effort. A month before the election Anthony wrote to Martha Wright that she still did not trust Stone and Blackwell, that she thought their real end in the supposed coalition effort was simply to secure the admission from Cady Stanton that she and Anthony had erred in their support of Train and Woodhull and their other actions. And, Anthony concluded, her friend had, unfortunately, given them all the assurances they wanted. In her diary Anthony attributed the failure of amalgamation to the Boston couple's unwillingness to work with her. Whatever the reasons, ambivalence characterized Cady Stanton's relationship with Anthony and the NWSA for the rest of the century.

After the Woodhull affair, Cady Stanton never again willingly involved herself with notorious personalities, even though cases of divorce and adultery involving woman's legal and personal oppression were common. She confined her views on sexuality and her crusade for enlightened motherhood to her lyceum tours. Yet by late 1872 she was reluctantly drawn into the unforeseen Beecher-Tilton scandal. This celebrated case reopened the issue of free love, contributed to the conservative direction of the suffrage movement, and inspired Cady Stanton's last reform crusade—her campaign against organized religion.

In the last months of 1872, Victoria Woodhull made public the details of the alleged affair between Henry Ward Beecher and Elizabeth Tilton. Woodhull's action set in motion a series of events that deeply affected Cady Stanton's public life. Beecher and Theodore Tilton, both of whom lived in nearby Brooklyn, New York, were both her friends and fellow suffragists. Although Elizabeth Tilton had not been an activist, she had been associated with Anthony and Cady Stanton in choosing poetry for publication in *The Revolution.*

The alleged affair dated from the late 1860s, when Theodore Tilton was often away on speaking tours, and Beecher, unhappy in his marriage, began visiting the sympathetic Elizabeth Tilton for solace. Cady Stanton was among the first of their friends to learn about the illicit relationship; Theodore Tilton had confided in her in late 1870 after his wife had confessed to him. The affair was soon common knowledge among suffragists, since the volatile natures of the three persons involved prompted each to periodic confessions.

Like most woman's rights colleagues, Cady Stanton kept quiet because she feared the effect of revealing the affair on Beecher, the Tiltons, and the woman's rights movement. Besides, when she suggested that Tilton and his family leave Brooklyn, he assured her that he had Beecher completely in his power. She made the error, however, of discussing the affair with Victoria Woodhull during their initial meeting in the spring of 1871. The younger feminist had already heard references to it at the 1871 NWSA Washington convention and had learned the details from Cady Stanton's longtime associate, Paulina Wright Davis. Cady Stanton confirmed what Woodhull already knew.

As long as Woodhull retained the support of woman's rights advocates, she, too, remained silent. But Cady Stanton's support of Grant and her own personal and financial difficulties induced Woodhull to detail what she knew about the affair in a special edition of her newspaper. As supporting evidence she printed a brief, but nonetheless embarrassing, version of her 1871 conversation with Cady Stanton. To make matters worse, Cady Stanton felt that Woodhull had changed her statements so that they appeared coarse and unnecessarily graphic. "Whatever I said," she wrote to Anthony, "was clothed in refined language at least, however disgusting the subject."

She refused, however, to be drawn further into a situation that the guardians of morality viewed, in her words, as "prurient" and "nauseating," even after vice crusader Anthony Comstock brought suit against Woodhull under the obscenity statute which bore his name for her reporting of the affair. On her return from a lyceum tour shortly after Woodhull's revelations, Cady Stanton found a bushel of letters querying her about her involvement. She threw them all in the fire and answered none. Concerned for her own reputation and for that of the woman's movement, she continued to remain silent. In 1874 she refused to testify before a committee of Beecher's church which investigated Woodhull's charges.

Only when it became apparent that Elizabeth Tilton was being made a public scapegoat for Beecher did Cady Stanton speak out. Elizabeth Tilton's actions were confusing. For several years after the end of the affair she remained with her husband, apparently reconciled with him. Just before the 1874 church investigation, however, she left him. At the inquiry she denied that the affair with Beecher had occurred. But by this point, after anxious years of intricate manipulations to keep the affair secret, everyone's actions had become erratic. Some authorities think that Theodore Tilton had an affair with Victoria Woodhull in the summer of 1871, after he had sought her out to persuade her to keep quiet. Woodhull even insinuated that she had had some sort of liaison with Henry Ward Beecher.

Beecher continued to declare himself innocent. He still had considerable influence over Elizabeth Tilton. His florid romanticism attracted many women, and he had been her pastor since her youth. She was a dependent personality, easily persuaded by Beecher's supporters that she ought not destroy him, a celebrated spokesman of the nation's values, for the sake of a possibly unfaithful husband. Enmeshed in a web of prevarications and apprehensive that Tilton might file suit in civil court, Beecher asserted in his final defense before the church enquiry that Elizabeth Tilton, not he, was the guilty party. Now he claimed that she had thrown herself at him and that he had steadfastly resisted her advances. To bolster his assertions, Beecher and his associates launched an attack on the suffragists. They charged that association with the free love views of the NWSA leadership had undermined the morality of both Theodore and Elizabeth Tilton. Beecher even included in the indictment his suffragist sister Isabella Beecher Hooker, dismissing her as insane when she joined his critics.

Cady Stanton could no longer keep silent over what she viewed as a "holocaust of womanhood." First Victoria Woodhull, then Elizabeth Tilton, and finally she herself along with the entire woman's movement were being unfairly vilified. She attacked Beecher directly. She minced no words in presenting him as the slave of his own reputation and of his own and others' considerable financial interests in his church, his religious newspaper, and his writings—all of which would be jeopardized if he admitted his guilt. A group of wealthy men insulate Beecher, she wrote, "a faithful, protecting band, not loving truth and justice less, but their own pockets more." She castigated Beecher for labeling the suffragists "human hyenas" and "free lovers" and for using Elizabeth Tilton like a "football." "What statements and counterstatements they have wrung from her unwilling lips; then like a withered flower, 'the Great Preacher' casts her aside and tells the world 'she thrust her affection' upon him unsought."

Yet Cady Stanton tried to place herself above vituperation. She praised Elizabeth Tilton's courage and independence in finally leaving her husband for the man she loved and thereby revealing "a touch of grand womanhood." Above all, to her the affair illustrated the need for liberalized divorce laws. "If it be proven that such men as Henry Ward Beecher and Theodore Tilton find the marriage laws of the State of New York too stringent, both being in discordant marriage relations, might it not be well to review the laws, as well as their violations?"

In the end, Cady Stanton's writings about the affair served little purpose beyond easing her own conscience. Even Henry Stanton, who rarely intervened in her activities during these years, appealed to Susan Anthony (who refused to comment publicly on the affair) to persuade his wife to desist. So much had been written on all sides by the time Cady Stanton added her commentary that the public was confused over who was guilty and innocent. And conservative suffragists were outraged by her arguments for liberalized divorce and her support of Elizabeth Tilton's leaving her husband.

Shortly after the church investigation, which exonerated Beecher, Tilton himself filed civil charges for alienation of his wife's affections. The trial occupied the winter and spring of 1875, and once again the free love charges were dragged through the press. Fearful of what the suffragists might reveal, neither prosecution nor defense called Anthony or Cady Stanton to the stand. Nor did either side allow Elizabeth Tilton to give testimony—an action which reflected their joint fear of what she might say but which infuriated Cady Stanton. Like Abby Sage in the McFarland-Richardson trial, Elizabeth Tilton was not allowed to defend herself by giving her version of the affair in court. In the end, the jury reached no verdict, and Tilton did not further pursue the matter.

The affair changed the lives of most of those involved in it. Both Theodore and Elizabeth Tilton, permanently separated, were ruined. She lived with a relative and quietly raised their children. Her nerves shattered, she died after reversing her earlier testimony and admitting the truth of the affair in a public letter. Theodore Tilton spent the rest of his long life in Paris, doing little besides playing chess in public cafes. Victoria Woodhull, now penniless, was acquitted of Anthony Comstock's charge of sending indecent material through the mail, but soon thereafter underwent a religious conversion, repudiated her free love views, and took up permanent residence in England. Eventually she married a titled and wealthy Englishman. She surfaced briefly in Cady Stanton's life when she visited her former ally in England to request a character reference for her prospective husband's family. Only Henry Ward Beecher survived the storm of criticism and continued his career apparently unscathed. As for Cady Stanton and Anthony, they had now to face another substantial free love charge. The result was further to deepen the commitment of the NWSA to narrow political goals—a more conservative orientation to which Cady Stanton initially acquiesced but against which she would later rebel.

The 1876 centennial anniversary of the American Revolution offered an opportunity for woman's rights forces to counter Beecher's free love charges by recasting their image in a political mold. The centennial observance centered on a huge exposition, held in Philadelphia. Women members of the exposition's planning board had successfully demanded the erection of a special woman's building, but its exhibits did not include a display on the woman's rights movement. Overlooked, NWSA leaders set up their own exhibit in downtown Philadelphia.

They also determined to take advantage of July Fourth special observances, which were another highlight of the centennial year, by having declarations of woman's rights read during local festivities and in the national celebration in Independence Hall, Philadelphia. Fearful that Cady Stanton, still the movement's outstanding writer, might refuse to draft the Philadelphia declaration if she were solicited by letter, Anthony deputized Matilda Jocelyn Gage, then NWSA president, to see her friend in person. She knew that Cady Stanton, however alienated from the NWSA, could not refuse a personal appeal. The approach was successful, and Cady Stanton took the major part in writing the document. Although the denial of the suffrage was its central focus, the declaration assailed other discriminations. Using the Andrew Johnson impeachment as example, Cady Stanton submitted "articles of impeachment" against the nation's rulers, including unequal law codes, the absence of women from juries, taxation of women without representation, and universal manhood suffrage with its perpetuation of an aristocracy of sex. She argued that women, like men, had defended liberty since the nation's early days and deserved recognition on the Fourth of July. Finally, she referred to her ideas about the dangers of woman's dependence and the need for enlightened motherhood. "Woman's degraded, helpless position is the weak point in our institutions today," she wrote, "severing family ties, filling our asylums with the deaf, the dumb, the blind; our prisons with criminals, our cities with drunkenness and prostitution; our homes with disease and death."

In contrast to the 1848 Seneca Falls declaration, the document did not have a lasting impact. It stood out neither for felicity of phrasing nor dramatic appeal. The argument was complex, the tone lawyerlike. The statement was a reasoned brief, not an impassioned manifesto. But it served a useful purpose. When centennial officials refused the NWSA a featured place in the Philadelphia July Fourth celebration, a delegation gained entrance to Independence Hall, presented the declaration to the presiding officer, and then, proceeding outside the hall, found an empty bandstand from which Susan Anthony read the declaration to an assembled crowd.

Despite her authorship of the 1876 declaration, Cady Stanton did not take part in the Independence Hall protest but instead read the document aloud in a subsequent indoor rally. Surprisingly, she attributed her absence from the kind of militant protest she often had advocated to the fact that she was growing old. "Some of our younger coadjutors," she wrote "decided to take the risk of a public insult." Yet although she was sixty-one in 1876, she was still active on the lyceum circuit. And, although her weight made physical activity increasingly difficult, she still scoffed at illness and prided herself on an excellent constitution.

More than anything else, however, complaints about age reflected her alienation from the woman's movement and her continuing disappointment with the conservatism of younger, post-Civil War feminists. Major NWSA documents were still delegated to her for drafting, and Anthony still came periodically to her home for help in writing speeches and official statements. In 1874 she had stumped the state of Michigan in a NWSA campaign for a state suffrage amendment. At Washington conventions and May meetings she was often a featured speaker. But Anthony was dominant in the organization, and the younger women supported her. Among them Anthony was known as "Aunt Susan," Cady Stanton was always "Mrs. Stanton." Anthony's supporters were often critical of Cady Stanton, charging, for example, that her enthusiasms were counterproductive. "Mrs. Stanton's *greatest delight*," wrote Harriet Taylor Upton, "was to spring some quite radical statement on the assemblage . . . something that would 'set them on their ears' . . . confounding poor Susan and causing setbacks to the Cause." For her part, Cady Stanton tried to keep her discontent to herself. "As I usually preserve the exterior of a saint there is no use of everybody knowing how like a fallen angel I often feel."

Yet the centennial of 1876 marked a rapprochement between Cady Stanton and the NWSA. The celebration of the revolution to which she claimed special kinship thrilled her. She enjoyed the comradeship established at the NWSA display in Philadelphia, a temporary headquarters where suffragists planned strategy and worked long hours writing and distributing publicity. During the centennial year she once again consented to serve as NWSA president.

In addition, she played an important role in implementing the new NWSA strategy to which the Philadelphia protest of

1876 had given impetus. In 1875 the Supreme Court, in Minor *versus* Happersett, had ruled against the suffragist argument that the Fourteenth Amendment enfranchised women. The new departure policy thus met an insuperable barrier. In its place, the NWSA in 1877 revived its earlier plan of constitutional revision through a sixteenth, woman suffrage, amendment and mounted a new petition campaign to Congress. That same year, while lecturing in California, Cady Stanton conferred with California Senator Aaron Sargeant, a woman suffrage supporter who agreed to reintroduce the amendment into Congress. Cady Stanton probably drafted the new version of the amendment, although it later became known as the Susan B. Anthony amendment—a tribute both to Anthony's tireless activity in its behalf and to suffragist loyalty to her. In 1878 Cady Stanton was once again elected president of the NWSA, a position she would hold until the merger of the NWSA and the AWSA in 1890 and then until 1892 for the united NAWSA.

Between 1877 and 1890 Cady Stanton supported the NWSA policy of lobbying Congress for passage of the constitutional amendment. From time to time she gave testimony in its behalf before congressional committees. Her own experiences in the unsuccessful state suffrage campaigns in Kansas in 1867 and in Michigan in 1874 had convinced her that the voters were less enlightened than their legislators. None of the eight popular referendums held to secure state suffrage amendments between 1870 and 1890 succeeded. State legislators, by comparison, were responsible for almost every advance in woman's rights during the century, including property rights for married women, suffrage in school elections (granted in nineteen states by 1890), and the general right to vote (made lawful in three states by 1890). Even Henry Blackwell and Lucy Stone, after an 1882 defeat in Nebraska, decided that the AWSA should concentrate on lobbying legislatures rather than on mass campaigns among the general population.

Given the limited resources of the NWSA, whose membership before the 1880s was smaller than the AWSA, concentrating effort on federal legislators rather than state representatives made good sense. At the federal level, success in lobbying was as much related to energy and initiative as to size of organization; there, suffrage speeches received free distribution through the *Congressional Record;* and sympathetic members of Congress would send out publicity under the franking privilege. Cady Stanton was optimistic about these lobbying efforts, noting by the mid-1880s that committee rooms formerly empty were full when suffrage leaders gave testimony, that congressmen and senators attended NWSA receptions, and that members of Congress even came to the January Washington suffrage conventions. NWSA leaders also sent delegations to professional gatherings, and, every four years, to political party conventions, although the two major parties for the most part ignored them. Cady Stanton did not take part in these delegations, nor, after her efforts for Grant in 1872, did she participate in any presidential campaign.

At times the work of lobbying was hard and unpleasant. Cady Stanton remembered her 1878 testimony before the Senate Committee on Privileges and Elections as the worst experience of her speaking career. She stood before a committee of men much younger than herself, all of whom were seated in armchairs. The chairman, studiously avoiding paying attention to her, read the newspaper, stared at the ceiling, sharpened his pencil, and jumped up to open and close windows and doors to prevent her from establishing rapport with the members.

Yet the lobbying itself, along with the renewal of resolve after the centennial, spurred a sizable growth in NWSA state organizations in the 1880s. Before the mid-1880s, the AWSA had been dominant within the states and had achieved notable success in persuading state legislatures to grant woman suffrage in school elections. By the middle years of the decade the position of the two organizations was reversed, even though the AWSA enjoyed the financial backing of Henry Blackwell and published a long-lived magazine, *The Woman's Journal.* Yet the NWSA, with limited funds and only occasional short-lived

journals founded by enterprising members, outdistanced its
Boston rival, a tribute to the congressional lobbying effort,
which provided a national rallying point. More importantly,
NWSA dominance reflected Anthony's organizational genius,
her lobbying skills, and her extraordinary vigor.

Slow but steady progress in congressional support was registered between 1872 and 1890. In 1882 each house appointed
a Select Committee on Woman Suffrage, and both committees
reported the measure favorably to the floor of the parent body.
The bill was actually debated on the floor of the Senate and
brought to a vote, though a negative one, in 1886. In 1891,
however, Susan Anthony, the organization's chief lobbyist,
moved her permanent home to Rochester. Two years later the
combined NAWSA, under pressure from western delegates
who disliked the long journey to Washington, abandoned the
policy of lobbying Congress in favor of state action. After 1896
Congress no longer considered the measure.

Progress in the suffrage campaign was slow, and Cady Stanton was not by nature patient. She had become sufficiently
reconciled to Anthony and the suffrage cause by 1876 to accept the titular presidency of the movement, although its over-
all direction was probably not one that she would have chosen.
But her attempt in the 1860s to center woman's rights on
marriage and divorce had not succeeded. The failure of the
Woodhull involvement underscored even more the difficulties
for radicalism in a society becoming increasingly conservative.
By the 1870s labor unions were in decline; business leaders
were paramount in politics and the economy; Congress and
the courts ignored the laws guaranteeing black rights; Anthony Comstock and the conservative wing of the social purity
movement enforced rigid moral standards; and an anti-woman
suffrage society appeared in 1871, the membership of which
would ultimately outdistance that of the suffrage organizations.

Above all, moderate woman's organizations like the woman's clubs which dated from 1868 and the Women's Christian
Temperance Union, founded in 1874, were the principal ben-

eficiaries of woman's postwar interest in broader public roles. Cady Stanton realized the potential strength of these organizations as early as 1873, when she appeared on the organizing program of the American Association for the Advancement of Women, founded by moderates partly to counter any notion that Victoria Woodhull and free love ideas represented organized women. Few of these groups directly espoused woman's rights. Yet areas of common concern existed between them and the NWSA on certain reform issues, particularly in their opposition to continuing attempts to legalize prostitution. On this issue NWSA and WCTU auxiliaries and even the woman's clubs, increasingly drawn to social reform rather than self-improvement, forged successful coalitions.

Cady Stanton often asserted that apathy was feminism's major obstacle, and she realized the potential of these diverse organizations for awakening women to a sense of oppression. Sometimes woman's clubs and the WCTU were useful allies in state suffrage campaigns, as their leaders came to consider the vote important in achieving social reform. The WCTU officially endorsed woman suffrage in 1881. Temperance and Christian morality were its main goals, and officially it held domesticity to be woman's proper role. Yet its charismatic and farseeing president, Frances Willard, shaped a broad program for the organization and held the conservatives under control until her death in 1898. Willard's energy and organizational genius were the equal of Anthony's, and the two women had a warm working relationship.

Cady Stanton was wary of the temperance work of the WCTU. The parallel to antebellum temperance organizations, whose conservatism had surfaced when she sought to lead them in the direction of feminism, was obvious. Still, Willard's control of the WCTU seemed as strong as Anthony's control of the NWSA. Although WCTU involvement in state suffrage campaigns roused the opposition of the powerful liquor industry, the support of the nation's largest organization of women was important. Neither Willard nor temperance "harms us a particle," Cady Stanton wrote in 1880.

By the 1880s Cady Stanton had come to view the program of the woman's movement from varying perspectives. Upon occasion she exulted in the success of achieving such gains as improved legal rights and entry into the professions. "To contrast our position thirty years ago, under the old common law of England, with that we occupy under the advanced legislation of to-day," she wrote in 1878, "is enough to assure us that we ... already see the mile-stones of a new civilization." At other times gloom pervaded her discussions of the discrimination still existing and the gradual pace of change. "Society is based on this fourfold bondage of woman—Church, State, Capital and Society," she wrote in 1888, "making liberty and equality for her antagonistic to every organized institution."

Her bifurcated perspective in these years reflected her underlying disaffection. More and more she functioned not as a movement strategist but as an interpreter of the policies of others. To a great extent she had become a figurehead. Universally praised for her oratory and writing, she was revered as the NWSA's founder and honored as its senior stateswoman. But her supporters within the NWSA were in the minority. Even Anthony kept tight rein on her. In 1882, for example, Anthony dissuaded her from sending official congratulations to Frederick Douglass on his marriage to a white woman because of the negative public attitude toward intermarriage.

Her autobiography subtly stressed her disaffection during these years. Written in 1897, when she felt much rancor against the NWSA, whose younger leaders in her view had refused her advice and treated her disrespectfully, it paid almost no attention to her work for the suffrage movement after the Philadelphia exposition. She indicated rather that she had spent her time, aside from lecturing and attending the Washington NWSA conventions, in the festivities associated with the college graduations and marriages of her sons and daughters, in socializing with old friends in Tenafly and New York City, and in several long trips to England and France.

For Cady Stanton to maintain a compromise position was

impossible. She had long viewed herself as a radical who presented striking new issues to stir women up and produce new resolve. In the 1880s her interest moved in a surprising new direction: she attempted to gain NWSA support for a campaign against traditional Christianity. This time, however, her campaign failed. She ended the last decades of her life with the admiration of all but in isolation from the movement she once had led.

Before she resigned the presidency of the NAWSA in 1892, Cady Stanton performed two additional services. The first task was to edit, between 1880 and 1885, three volumes of the documentary *History of Woman Suffrage,* in collaboration with Susan Anthony and with the help of Matilda Jocelyn Gage. Her second service for the organized suffrage movement was to participate in the founding of the International Council of Women, in 1888.

Both Cady Stanton and Anthony had contemplated writing a history of the suffrage movement for some time. For years, in her meticulous fashion, Anthony had collected every possible document, intending to use her archive as a basis for a history. The division of the movement in 1869 made the project even more imperative. The AWSA regularly issued *The Woman's Journal,* whereas, after the demise of *The Revolution* in 1870, Anthony and Cady Stanton had no journal of their own. Unequal documentation could lead future historians to infer that the American organization had been more important than the National and that Lucy Stone was the founder and most important figure of the movement. In addition, male historians might play down the movement's importance or overlook it entirely.

Working together again on a congenial project appealed to both women. As always, Anthony was in charge of research, while Cady Stanton wrote the narrative passages. They lived together while writing the history, completing the first two volumes at Cady Stanton's house at Tenafly and the last one at the old Cady home in Johnstown. Occasionally the intimacy of their work inspired them to take the partnership into the field once again, as much, it seems, for the pleasure of working together as for any lasting effect. On Election Day, November 2, 1880, a Republican party wagon stopped by the Tenafly house to take eligible male voters to the polls. With her husband and sons absent, Cady Stanton announced that she owned the house and paid the taxes on it and would vote herself. She and Anthony went to the polls and intimidated the election officials into allowing Cady Stanton to vote. In Johnstown they successfully campaigned for the election of a woman to the school board and organized a suffrage society with Cady Stanton as president.

Such activities were a welcome break in the intense work of writing the history. During the seven months in which they wrote the first volume they took no time off, except for an occasional evening in New York City and a few days in Washington for the annual NWSA convention. Cady Stanton complained about Anthony's rigorous schedule; Anthony complained about her friend's love of visiting and socializing. Yet, as they generally had throughout their years together, each kept her dissatisfactions under control. When they disagreed too vehemently, Margaret Stanton remembered, one or both of them would get up from the table where they worked and go out into the garden to cool down.

They had first begun to work on the history in 1876, soon after the Centennial Exposition. In the beginning they visualized it as a brief synopsis of 100 pages or so on the order of a widely distributed pamphlet that Anthony had written on her 1872 voting trial. In fact, Anthony had offered the projected short work as a premium to anyone who made a financial contribution for NWSA centennial activities. But they soon decided they could not do justice to their theme in such abbreviated space. Nor did their schedules allow them the time necessary to produce a lengthy volume. For the time being they abandoned the project, although they continued on their own to solicit reminiscences and documents from leaders of the movement.

By 1880 the two women felt the pressure of time: Anthony was sixty and Cady Stanton sixty-five. Cady Stanton retired that year from lyceum lecturing and had free time available. As they worked on the history, its size came to exceed their expectations. The first volume, 871 pages in length, covered only the years between 1848 and 1861. But they had decided to publish all possible speeches and reminiscences. They kept Cady Stanton's explanatory passages brief in order to let the documents speak for themselves.

Considering the amount of their materials and the fact that they had neither stenographers nor copyists to assist them, the history was a prodigious writing feat. Once they had chosen and edited the documents and Cady Stanton had written the intervening narratives, they had to check the text for accuracy and copy it in a neat hand for the printers. Before the final printing, they had to read and check proof. Following a common practice of the time, each chapter was printed as soon as the text was ready, a procedure which speeded up production but damaged continuity of argument and thematic development.

Rather than a disciplined historical analysis, the history is a potpourri of extraordinary information revealing the complexity and strengths of the nineteenth-century woman's movement. The work was written as a tool of information and persuasion for nineteenth-century minds and, incidentally, to prove the primacy of the suffrage movement over other, competing reforms. Excerpts from Cady Stanton's speeches reveal her ideas about birth control and enlightened motherhood, but from the narrative she appears thoroughly committed to suffrage reform and the policies of the NWSA. Thus far had her reconciliation with the suffrage movement proceeded as well as her desire to demonstrate a united front to the outside, predominantly antifeminist world.

In the years after the 1869 division, the history focused almost exclusively on the NWSA. The two authors asked Lucy Stone to contribute a history of the AWSA, but she refused. Annoyed, they decided simply to omit the AWSA, until Harriot Stanton Blatch persuaded them that they would be open to criticism for bias. In the end Blatch herself wrote a short chapter on the development of the AWSA.

Beginning with modest expectations for the project, Anthony became so committed that she used sizable portions of her own funds to subsidize it, including a $25,000 legacy left her for woman's rights by a Boston woman. Ultimately, Anthony bought out Cady Stanton's financial share in the project so that she might distribute the history free to libraries and influential individuals. After the third volume was published in 1886, Cady Stanton ended her collaboration, characteristically giving her age as the reason for withdrawing. Privately she revealed that she could no longer tolerate the tedium of editing it. And, given her general dissatisfaction with the suffrage movement, other, more congenial projects had come to interest her. With the assistance of Ida Husted Harper, Anthony published two more lengthy volumes before her death in 1906.

Anthony and Cady Stanton also worked together in the 1880s to forge an international woman's organization. Nineteenth-century reformers often participated in international organizations and crossed the seas for international conferences, as Cady Stanton herself had in 1840. Her own interest in internationalism revived in the 1880s when both her son, Theodore, and her daughter, Harriot, went to France to study, married Europeans, and for several decades lived abroad— Theodore in France and Harriot in England. Of her seven children, Cady Stanton was closest to these two, both of whom as adults shared her interest in woman's rights. Harriot was an activist, first in England and, after her husband's death, in New York. Theodore was a newpaperman and scholar, and in 1878 he served as the official NWSA representative to an International Woman's Rights Congress in Paris. As a result of this meeting, an international committee was formed. Although both Anthony and Cady Stanton were named to it, the committee played no role in their subsequent efforts toward internationalism.

In 1882, after finishing the second volume of the history, Cady Stanton paid her first visit to Europe since 1840. She needed a vacation, was disenchanted with suffrage politics, and wanted to spend time with her children. She stayed first with Theodore and helped him edit his *Woman Question in Europe,* a product of his feminism and internationalism. She then accompanied her daughter to England, where Harriot married a well-to-do English landowner. Cady Stanton reacquainted herself with old friends there and made new ones. This time, however, she was not in her husband's shadow. Now seventy-seven years of age and in poor health, Henry Stanton did not accompany her on her trips to Europe. Cady Stanton was feted as a famed American in her own right. English feminists sought her counsel, and she gave them advice on their current campaign for a married woman's property bill, which, in fact, Parliament enacted that same year.

During her time abroad, Cady Stanton discussed founding an international woman's organization with continental and English feminists. In 1883 Anthony joined her both for a vacation and to add her voice to the international efforts. Yet it was not until a farewell reception the day Cady Stanton and Anthony sailed together back to the United States that they were able to persuade English leaders to join them in a planning committee.

However, the idea of founding an international woman's organization—which had seemed simple in England—became complex with an ocean between potential members and with the indecision of British leaders. After a number of years Anthony simply took the task into her own hands. In 1887 the AWSA made overtures toward uniting the two organizations, and 1888 marked the fortieth anniversary of the Seneca Falls convention. It was the moment for a gala celebration and a display of suffragist strength and unity.

Rather than focusing just on suffrage, which had been the original plan, the agenda for the founding meeting included the broad spectrum of woman's political and social concerns. Because of the distance and the stormy ocean crossing that spring, only seven European women appeared. But women attending represented countries as various as England, France, Norway, Denmark, Finland, and India. Representatives of most American woman's organizations were there, including Jane Cunningham Croly, president of Sorosis, Frances Willard of the WCTU, and Leonora Barry, the workingwoman secretary of the Knights of Labor. According to one observer, "Not one of the most eminent women citizens had stayed away." Between sessions the delegates congregated in the hotel lobby, exchanging information and pictures of their children and families, making friends. President Grover Cleveland and the Senate committee on woman suffrage held receptions for them.

Before the meetings closed, both a permanent International Council of Women and a National Council of Women for the United States were established in an impressive effort to effect a broad coalition of all woman's organizations. Yet neither organization in the long run was particularly effective. They primarily functioned as informal fact-finding agencies, and over the years their meetings were neutral places for debate. In the twentieth century, the hope for forceful, successful international organizations of all women directed toward their rights remained a constant but unrealized dream.

Cady Stanton took little part in the actual preparations for the 1888 convocation, except to urge her English friends to attend. Although she was scheduled to give the opening and closing addresses, she fulfilled the obligation only after Susan Anthony wrote her a blistering letter demanding her presence and, when she had arrived in Washington, sequestered her in a hotel room to write her speech. Cady Stanton fully supported the formation of the international council, but by 1888 her disaffection with Anthony and the American suffrage movement had surfaced again. At times she contemplated permanent residence in England. Yet in the end her remarks before the convention were a brilliant display of her feminist ideas and her unsurpassed oratorical skill. Her closing statement appropriately proclaimed that women would create an internationalism that would triumph over all other ideologies. "In every country," she declared, "we see the wisest statesmen at their wits end vainly trying to meet the puzzling questions of the hour: in Russia, it is nihilism; in Germany, socialism; in France, communism; in England, home rule for Ireland . . . and in America, land, labor, taxes, tariffs, temperance and woman suffrage. Where shall we look for the new power whereby the race can be lifted up?" Her answer was clear. Drawing on the feminist ideas of a lifetime, she proclaimed that in woman's hands lay the hope of the future.

The Final Years:
Religion and Cooperation
1880–1902

In 1895, on the occasion of Cady Stanton's eigh-
tieth birthday, Susan Anthony arranged an extraordinary celebration. For the event, Anthony rented the New York City
Metropolitan Opera House. The auditorium was decorated in
baroque display. Banners and flowers festooned the boxes.
Massive scenic columns gave the stage the appearance of a
palatial throne room. On it, the organizers erected a dais with
three massive gold and velvet chairs crowned by an arch of
white flowers, with the name "Stanton" worked into the center
in pink flowers. The center chair was reserved for Cady Stanton, the other two for Anthony and Mary Lowes Dickinson,
president of the National Council of Women. It was, according
to Dickinson, a triumphant throne for a "queen among
women."

The birthday ceremony was as elaborate as its setting.
Friends and associates delivered tribute after tribute. A series
of tableaux, entitled "Then and Now," illustrated the changes
in woman's position over fifty years. Lights were dimmed, and
the names of the century's outstanding women flashed in
bright letters on a screen. Cady Stanton was showered with
gifts ranging from a grand piano to a hand embroidered nightgown.

Susan Anthony knew her friend well. Although such a pag-
eant on her own behalf would have embarrassed Anthony, she

had calculated the splendor to appeal to Cady Stanton's vanity and her love of display. She also meant to assuage Cady Stanton's alienation from the NAWSA and her envy of Anthony's now paramount position in it. Although Cady Stanton was hurt that the National Council of Women rather than the NAWSA sponsored the event, still the tribute touched her. "Having been accustomed for half a century to blame rather than praise," she wrote, "I was surprised with such a manifestation of approval."

Her surprise was warranted. She had played little part in the merger negotiations between the National and the American Suffrage Associations in 1890. Within two years she resigned the post of president to which she had been elected at Anthony's insistence. She could no longer tolerate the organization's sole commitment to suffrage nor the younger members' hostility. "The National has been growing political and conservative for some time," she wrote in 1888. "Lucy and Susan alike see suffrage only. They do not see woman's religious and social bondage, neither do the young women in either organization."

The speech which she delivered on the occasion of her resignation was a thinly veiled statement of her discontent. Entitled "The Solitude of Self," the speech revealed—as her writings often did—as much about her personal sentiments as about her ideology. She reiterated her commitment to individual rights and expanded on what she considered life's meaning, particularly her overwhelming sense of the ultimate solitude of the human condition. "Our inner being which we call ourself, no eye nor touch of man or angel has ever pierced," she wrote. Despite her love of socializing and her many friends and large family, she chose to depict the human situation as that of Robinson Crusoe on a desert island, with only a woman Friday for a companion. The great lesson that nature seemed to teach, she concluded, "is self-dependence, self-protection, self-support." After 1892 she never again attended a NAWSA convention.

The major disagreement between Cady Stanton and her NAWSA critics in these years centered around her attempts to initiate a crusade against organized religion. From 1878 on she attempted each year to persuade the NWSA to condemn the antifeminism of the Bible and Christian creeds and religion's discrimination against women. And, beginning in 1882, she sought to organize a committee of women scholars and activist feminists to undertake a revised feminist version of the Bible.

Despite her adult agnosticism, she had never entirely emancipated herself from the theology of her childhood or from the pervasive evangelicalism of her early maturity. In later years she observed a woman using a thick Bible to raise the height of a chair seat for a child. She could not stop feeling that this action was blasphemous, even though it was "long after my reason had repudiated ... [the Bible's] divine authority." Evangelical millennialism and the Puritan emphasis on self-control permeated her utopian ideology. As a lyceum lecturer intent on converting her listeners to feminism, her function was strikingly ministerial. She often spoke in churches and occasionally preached Sunday sermons. When she stayed in local homes, her hosts invariably asked her to give the blessing at mealtime, as though she were a minister who had come to dinner. She devised a feminist prayer which asked for grace from the heavenly Mother as well as the Father and praised the woman who cooked the meal rather than, as was customary, the man who provided the money for it. "Heavenly Father and Mother," the blessing went, "make us thankful for all the blessings of this life and ever mindful of the patient hands that oft in weariness set our tables and prepare our food. For humanity's sake, Amen."

In the 1880s she visited William Henry Channing, an expatriate Unitarian minister and former reform associate then in his seventies and residing in London. She was amazed to learn that he and other early Unitarian rebels had come again to accept Christian views of eternity they had once rejected. Un-

knowingly, Anthony provided a reason for her friend's renewed interest in religion when she attributed the Unitarians'
surprising return to traditionalism to their advanced ages.
Older woman's rights associates were also finding new meaning in creeds and confessions, although not always traditional
ones. In their later years Elizabeth Smith Miller, Isabella
Beecher Hooker, and Matilda Jocelyn Gage found assurance
in spiritualism, a belief system which presumes that the living
can communicate with the dead. Cady Stanton rejected
spiritualism as farfetched, although she was attracted by
theosophy, a related religious philosophy stressing individual
growth and explaining human development along pseudo-
scientific, Comtean lines.

Cady Stanton's alarm over continued religious antifeminism
and the power of the male clergy also motivated her crusade
against organized religion. She saw little retreat in the influence of Christianity or the authority of ministers in late nineteenth-century America. After 1865, church membership and
attendance were on the increase. Although revivalism had died
out in the middle-class Calvinist churches of Cady Stanton's
youth, it was still strong in fundamentalist and lower-class
churches. Missionary, Bible, and tract societies were growing
in numbers and membership, and by midcentury powerful
new organizations like the YMCA and the Sunday schools had
appeared. Cady Stanton often complained that church property was not taxed and that ministers were given free houses,
free clothes, and free professional services. "All men pay more
respect to the black coat than any other," she wrote.

Occasionally Cady Stanton acknowledged Protestant flexi-
bility and the receptivity of some ministers to feminism. She
herself had preached in enough pulpits to be aware of clerical
support. In 1874, during her speaking tour of Michigan on
behalf of a woman suffrage referendum, she enthusiastically
noted that ministers of all denominations invited her to speak
on suffrage in place of their Sunday sermons. "Sitting Sunday
after Sunday in the different pulpits with reverend gentlemen
. . . I could not help thinking of the distance we had come since

that period in civilization when Paul's word was law. . . . " In 1883, after preaching in a London pulpit on the topic, "Has the Christian Religion Done Aught to Elevate Women?" she admitted privately that, although her sermon had focused on the negative, a strong case could be made for a positive interpretation.

Still she chose to stress clerical resistance, rather than accommodation. As early as the 1850s she had accused the Protestant clergy of being responsible for the factionalization of the antislavery movement and the ouster of women delegates from the 1840 London antislavery convention. In 1881 she charged that, with the exception of the Unitarians, the Universalists, and the liberal Quakers, "every sect holds a hostile attitude toward woman's equal status as a church member." In her view Henry Ward Beecher's power over Elizabeth Tilton was symbolic of the power of most ministers over their women parishioners, and his attacks on suffragists were characteristic of ministers' general antifeminism. "The *History of Woman Suffrage*," she wrote Theodore Stanton, "will be a terrible record for the clergy. Facts will show that no men, with few exceptions, behaved worse on our platform, and from no source did we have, and do we have to-day, such opposition as from them."

She now found the source of woman's subordination and dependence on men in religion's authority. "I have been traveling over the old world during the last few years and have found new food for thought," Cady Stanton wrote in 1885. "What power is it that makes the Hindu woman burn herself on the funeral pyre of her husband? Her religion. What holds the Turkish woman in the harem? Her religion. By what power do the Mormons perpetuate their system of polygamy? By their religion. Man, of himself, could not do this: but when he declares, 'Thus said the Lord,' of course he can do it. So long as ministers stand up and tell us that as Christ is the head of the church, so is man the head of the woman, how are we to break the chains which have held women down through the ages?"

The attitude of many religious women disturbed her even more. During her years on the lyceum circuit she had encountered intense and unexpected religious antifeminism among her audiences. Traveling through midwestern towns and spending time with average Americans brought her to the core of American religious culture. There she found, to her surprise, that audiences objected not to her birth control message but rather to the contradictions between her woman's rights doctrines and their own Christian beliefs. "For twelve years in succession I have travelled from Maine to Texas," she wrote in 1880, "trying by public lectures and private conversations 'to teach women to think.' But the chief obstacle in the way of success has everywhere been their false theology, their religious superstitions. . . . " She found the cant of Christian women the worst she had ever encountered, particularly since women, whom she expected to be the agents of utopia, constituted a majority of church members in nineteenth-century America. Whatever common-sense woman's rights propositions she advanced in her lectures, some woman invariably quoted Biblical passages in opposition.

At times she despaired, for it seemed to her that most men had emancipated themselves from the bondage of traditional dogmas, but women continued to defend the old antifeminist doctrines and allowed the church to exploit them as workers against their best interests. "Go into any little country town," she wrote, "and the women's chief excitement is to be found in church fairs and church decorating." Remembering how the fledgling minister she had helped support through seminary training preached a special sermon on woman's inferiority from the Johnstown pulpit, she consistently dressed down women who raised money for all-male theological seminaries or foreign missions instead of for the alleviation of poverty and other social ills at home. Moreover, she was amazed to find in her travels that women, not men, upheld the belief in the curse of Eve. For example, she was shocked to learn that many women refused during childbirth to take chloroform (then used to lessen labor pains) because they believed their pains were a part of woman's special burden inherited from Eve.

Intent on utopia, Cady Stanton had little tolerance for women who found satisfaction living woman's traditional roles in traditional ways. Centered on her vision of the ideal woman, who either abandoned domesticity or raised motherhood to new dimensions of individual and social reform, she did not understand the attractions of church fairs and the like to women who lived life as it was and found satisfaction where they could.

Her feminist interpretation of religion extended even to theology. In her view the predominance of women as church members had neither softened nor humanized Christian creeds but rather had reinforced Christianity's male-centered theology and its belief in a masculine, patriarchal God. By the 1890s she roughly outlined a feminist cosmology. In her view God was feminine as well as masculine, the apex of a system of male and female forces which permeated the universe and kept it in equilibrium. Among human beings, this system took the form of sexual attraction between men and women and provided that women were drawn to a patriarchal God and men to a maternal one. "The reason we have an exclusively male God," she declared, "is that our religion is . . . sustained mainly by women."

Cady Stanton's anticlerical crusade was meant not only to assail religious antifeminism but also to support those church-women who, like many secular women in post-Civil War America, questioned domesticity and demanded a larger involvement outside the home. Within the denominations, more and more women dominated the missionary field; this expansion represented one of the major developments of post-Civil War religion. Women were coming to control the majority of new missionary boards, despite the substantial opposition of men in every denomination. Baptist and Presbyterian women were increasingly allowed to speak in prayer meetings and at district conference gatherings, although in 1880 the Pan-Presbyterian Council contemptuously dismissed Cady Stanton's suggestion that it condemn the old dogmas about the natural inferiority of women. Women were studying theology in many institutions, and asking to be ordained as preachers, elders, and deacons, and to be admitted as delegates to church governing bodies. But in 1881 the Methodists abandoned their liberal policy of ordaining women as ministers, and joined Baptists, Episcopalians, Presbyterians, and Congregationalists in refusing officially to ordain women. Cady Stanton wanted the NWSA to support these religious women and to encourage their awareness of the general struggle.

Cady Stanton thought that an attack on organized religion made excellent political sense—or so she explained to Antoinette Brown Blackwell, whose support as the nation's first woman minister she wanted to secure. After half a century of suffrage agitation, Cady Stanton argued, politicians still paid little heed to the suffragists, but merely played with them, like a cat with a mouse. The suffragists' political campaign was exhausted; another new direction was needed. It was time to take on one of the basic sources of woman's oppression and to raise a new hornet's nest of publicity that would ultimately benefit the movement.

Yet the NWSA, increasingly influenced by the WCTU and conservative woman's clubs, refused to adopt her anticlerical declarations. Even Susan Anthony opposed them, arguing on one occasion that abolitionist attacks against American churches in the old days had been counterproductive and that feminist anticlericals were getting in the way of her own attempts to convert religious women to feminism. But Cady Stanton was not alone in her crusade. In both 1880 and 1885 she succeeded in gaining NWSA passage of mild resolutions of censure; and both editors of the leading western suffrage journals, Matilda Jocelyn Gage of the *National Citizen and Ballot Box* and Clara Berwick Colby of *The Woman's Tribune,* supported her anticlericalism. Both Colby and Gage, in fact, agitated the religious question before Stanton took it up and may have influenced the latter's decision to do so. In 1890 Gage asserted that for years Cady Stanton had told her that she was "sick of the song of suffrage," that "the church was the greatest enemy," and that after the suffrage history was finished she would join Gage in an anticlerical crusade. That same year,

Gage broke away from the NAWSA to found a Woman's National Liberal Union as a vehicle for her own campaign against organized religion.

Cady Stanton reserved the full force of her anticlericalism for her *Woman's Bible,* a project conceived as early as 1882 but brought to fruition in 1895. She regarded it first of all as a useful tool for seminary women and others in their conflicts with church fathers. But it was the opposition she encountered in her lyceum talks that especially drew her to study Biblical texts. Eventually she became expert at the kind of customary theological argument based on a superior ability to quote Biblical passages. Yet this scholasticism came to seem insufficient to her, for it failed to address the fundamental question of Biblical antifeminism. Even the symbolic interpretation of the Bible popular among liberal scholars seemed a halfway measure to her. She reacted strongly to the failure to take antifeminism into account in new Bible translations, particularly in the widely acclaimed Revised Version of 1881, publication of which was a direct spur to her decision to undertake a feminist Bible on her own.

She did not immediately proceed to work on the projected volume because she did not then regard religious antifeminism as so threatening as she would later. Nor for a long time did Cady Stanton oppose the unofficial alliance between the WCTU and the NWSA. Her attitude changed when, in the mid-1880s, religious conservatives, including members of the WCTU, mounted a campaign for a Congressional declaration that Christianity was the nation's official religion, sought the strict enforcement of Sunday closing laws, agitated for the teaching of Protestantism in public schools, and introduced religious topics into suffrage conventions. In 1888 Cady Stanton wrote to Anthony that the whole issue ought to be aired at the next convention—a suggestion to which Anthony was unsympathetic.

Gaining little support from NWSA leaders, Cady Stanton attempted through articles and speeches to combat the demands of the religious traditionalists. In 1893 religious conservatives attempted to force the closing of the Chicago World's Fair on Sundays. Cady Stanton claimed responsibility for having defeated their efforts by means of a leaflet which she wrote and of which she distributed 10,000 copies at her own expense. The issue of Sunday closing had long been central in the struggle between religious traditionalists and modernists. Conservatives saw it as a central means of stimulating sabbath observance; to Cady Stanton Sunday was the workers' one day of rest in what was often a six-day work week, and attractive recreation ought to be provided for them.

By 1895 *The Woman's Bible* could wait no longer. Cady Stanton initially envisioned the work as a new translation along feminist lines. But she could find no respected woman Greek or Hebrew scholar willing to risk her reputation on such a controversial project. Thus the work became a commentary on passages from the Bible—a form of exegesis long popular among scholars. Cady Stanton used the Revised Version and a translation by Julia Smith, a Connecticut woman, as texts. Smith's translation was not widely known, but she was legendary among feminists for having won several court cases over her refusal to pay property taxes because women were denied the vote.

Cady Stanton had intended her Scriptures to be the product of a committee of women, on the order of the male boards which produced the most respected Bible translations—and which excluded women. Yet even though she assembled a revising committee of about twenty-five to give legitimacy to the final product, she herself wrote most of it. The commentaries were more polemical than scholarly—an emphasis which reflected Cady Stanton's dislike of scholarship and her hope that the work might appeal to the general public. Given the length of the Bible, she only analyzed chapters which directly dealt with women. This excision eliminated, according to her calculations, about 90 percent of the Bible and made her task feasible in a short period of time.

For the most part her commentaries were critical. She boldly stated her belief that the Scriptures, particularly the Old Testament, were little more than a history of the Jewish nation and its mythology. She accepted neither the divinity of Christ nor the virginity of his mother, Mary, a doctrine which she excoriated as "a slur on all natural motherhood." She realized that the Bible depicted the lives of many noble women and men, especially Jesus Christ, whom she described as the "great leading Radical of his time." Yet too often in her view Biblical men and women demonstrated the worst, not the best, traits in human nature. The Hebrew nation of the Old Testament, in particular, was a patriarchal society of the worst sort; its history was a long record of "war, corruption, rapine, and lust"; and its God, jealous and vengeful, was a representation of masculinity in its most repellent form. "I know of no other books," she wrote, "that so fully teach the subjection and the degradation of woman."

Much of *The Woman's Bible* was idiosyncratic, reiterating feminist creeds that Cady Stanton had preached for decades. For instance, she stressed that the women of the Old Testament were chattels of fathers and husbands and pointed out parallels to woman's nineteenth-century situation. With her own era in mind, she criticized Biblical woman's lack of independence. She was particularly scornful of Hebrew women who raised funds to support male charities and male ministers. Social evils like polygamy and prostitution were common in the Hebrew record; she castigated contemporary social purity reformers who tried to stamp out these ills while extolling the Bible as an exemplary book for teaching morality.

For a long time Cady Stanton had disagreed with the common contention of conservative churchmen that Christianity had been responsible for the development of progressive and humanitarian social institutions, including the presumably favorable position of Western in comparison with Moslem and Chinese women. Rather, she argued, Christianity had extolled male celibacy and systematically degraded women, persecuting them almost exclusively as witches and holding them responsible for original sin because of Eve's purported transgression. She had earlier argued that the concepts of

Eve's curse and original sin had not become church dogma until the writings of St. Augustine in the fifth century, who emphasized them largely because of his youthful experiences with a prostitute. In *The Woman's Bible* she carried the analysis even further. The story of the expulsion from Eden was mythological, she argued, and women, rather than being cursed, in fact had been blessed historically as the originators and rulers of Amazonian societies which had existed for many centuries before men had wrested away control to construct patriarchal societies based on woman's subjection.

Against conservatives, she built on contemporary liberal Biblical scholarship to argue that there were two creation stories in the Book of Genesis. The better known version in the second chapter, in which God created Eve out of Adam's rib —an episode long cited as Scriptural justification for Eve's subordination—was, according to Cady Stanton, added by some "wily writer" devoted to the idea of male domination. The creation story in the first chapter, in which God created man and woman simultaneously and equally, was the true account. Moreover, a passage in that chapter stated that "male and female" were created in the "image of God," proving that the Godhead was both masculine and feminine. "Thus Scripture, as well as science and philosophy, declared the eternity and equality of sex."

The Woman's Bible was a monument to feminist religious polemical scholarship. Yet in both the religious and the feminist communities of her day, it was a failure. Religious leaders refused to take it seriously, while the NAWSA in 1896 went so far as officially to disavow any connection with the volume. This action hurt and infuriated Cady Stanton. To mollify her, Anthony brought to Cady Stanton's home Carrie Chapman Catt, a leader of the younger suffragists and an eventual president of the NAWSA who had been a member of Cady Stanton's revision committee. Catt explained to a stony faced Cady Stanton that the resolution had been introduced by the women who were bearing the brunt of the work in the field and who had constantly to defend the organization against the charge that the suffrage movement was irreligious. Catt asserted that the NAWSA leadership had no desire to censure what Cady Stanton wrote as an individual but only to make clear that the organization did not endorse the work.

The meeting was a standoff. With no understanding of Cady Stanton's own years in the field and the opposition she had met there, Catt came away with the impression that the older suffragist was a selfish woman, who had always gotten her own way and could accept neither defeat nor compromise. The real issue, however, was one of Cady Stanton's radicalism versus the conservatism of the others. Cady Stanton wanted to attack religious antifeminism at its roots; her NAWSA opponents wanted to moderate their message to meet the demands of the pious. Cady Stanton had again lost her battle; she understood this and was silent. The new generation of suffragists rejected anticlerical action as politically inexpedient. But in their overwhelming quest for suffrage, they temporized on religious as well as on other issues, making feminism the conservative and largely ineffective force it would become once suffrage was achieved after the First World War.

Cady Stanton's preoccupation with religion in the last decades of her life did not submerge other elements of her thought and action. She continued to write and speak on the subjects that had interested her in earlier years: marriage and divorce, coeducation, suffrage. Occasionally she published essays on prison reform, a topic that had interested her since childhood visits to the Johnstown jail. In line with her libertarianism and reformist penal ideology, she supported reeducating inmates and reintegrating them into society. Her penal analysis was often directly feminist. "Fear, coercion, punishment," she wrote, "are the masculine remedies for moral weakness." She assured the inmates of the Jackson, Michigan, state prison in 1874 that great changes in prison life would be effected when the mothers of the nation had a voice in making policy. There would then be "cheerful surroundings, inspiring influences," and the "education of moral and intellectual faculties."

In addition to religion, however, the problems of poverty

and class relations moved to the forefront of her reform interest in the 1880s and 1890s. Growing social and economic dislocation above all forced these issues upon her attention. Advancing industrialization was producing increasing disparities in wealth as well as strikes and other disorders that threatened the social fabric. Like many intellectuals of her age, Cady Stanton focused on the question of workers and employers, believing that to forget the interests of the laboring classes was to imperil the entire society.

Her long visits in the 1880s to England also drew her toward the social question. England had experienced relatively greater urbanization; its aristocratic class structure gave greater exposure to democratic failings; and Owenite communitarianism and the Chartist struggle to liberalize Parliament by means of massive petitions had established a respected radical tradition. In the United States, she spent her time lecturing or entertaining family and friends. In England she was a tourist eager to experience the intellectual ferment of liberal London. Her daughter Harriot's home in rural Blasingstoke was within easy access of London. She had entree into British intellectual circles through her fame as an American reformer and her daughter's position as an executive both of the Blasingstoke Women's Government Society and the London Fabian Society. She visited the exiled Russian anarchist, Prince Kropotkin; she attended the Temple of Humanity where English Comteans had put into operation Comte's quasireligious rituals; she went to Fabian meetings and theosophic gatherings; and she spent time with Virginia antislavery expatriate Moncure Conway, whose Unitarian church was a center for British religious radicals.

Three schools of thought especially influenced her in these decades: Fabian socialism, whose proponents sought control of the government through the electoral process for the promotion of social welfare and community ownership of production; the "social gospel," a religious ideology whose adherents wanted to redirect Christianity to focus on social questions; and most importantly, the theory of cooperation.

Originating in the efforts of utopian industrialist Robert Owen to promote social ownership and operation of farms and factories, nineteenth-century cooperation took a number of forms. Early in the century, egalitarian agrarian communities were established, especially in the United States. More cautious innovators founded producers' and consumers' cooperatives; in the United States Grangers, the Knights of Labor, and the Farmers' Alliances experimented with them. In England they were particularly popular, and in 1869 a British Cooperative Union had been founded to further such arrangements. During the 1880s and 1890s, a period of renewed reform interest in England as well as the United States, the notion of cooperation attracted British reformers influenced by the asceticism of John Ruskin and William Morris and the renewed pietism of church people attracted by the cooperative societies of the Pauline era.

Cooperation had interested Cady Stanton since her visits to Brook Farm in the 1840s. Robert Dale Owen, Robert Owen's son and the founder of the Indiana New Harmony Community, had been a friend during her New York days. In England she spent time with George Jacob Holyoake, a major exponent of the cooperative creed, and among her closest friends were Jacob Bright, one of its leading advocates, and his wife and sisters, active in the British woman's rights movement. Harriot Stanton Blatch experimented with cooperation by providing financial backing for a cooperative laundry for the tenants on her husband's estate. "My dream of the future is cooperation," wrote Cady Stanton in 1882.

Cady Stanton used the concept of cooperation in a number of ways. Sometimes she concentrated on the need for producer and consumer cooperatives. More often, she promoted the establishment of communes on the order of Brook Farm or of the famed Fourierist phalanx in Guise, France, an ongoing community of 1800 persons. Often her adherence to cooperation was feminist in intent, and she emphasized the sharing of cleaning, cooking, and child care. Foreshadowing the ideas identified with Charlotte Perkins Gilman, Cady Stanton advocated apartment complexes with communal restaurants and recreation rooms.

In the eclectic radicalism of Cady Stanton's later years there was no ideological consistency. Although some of the aspects of socialist communes attracted her, she was never a socialist. Her philosophical optimism and her personal love of comfort dulled the rage that might have propelled her toward militant or Marxist solutions. Nor was she invariably sympathetic to the working classes or to ethnic groups. She still regarded rape as a crime of working-class men. She now advocated birth control as much to reduce the size of working-class families as to liberate all women. From this Malthusian perspective, poverty was the result not so much of adverse circumstances but of a presumed worker propensity for self-indulgence. Her writings on education, which she still regarded as the potential leveler of the class structure, stressed the need to teach morality more than practical skills. The laboring class needed to be taught "the knowledge of good and evil" in order to be able to demand any sensible improvement in their environment.

Above all, her notion of cooperation took on an increasingly conservative coloration. She often proposed that, rather than creating a new society, reformers ought to concentrate on creating a new ethic based on the principle of cooperation among individuals and groups. The problem with capitalism, she concluded, was not so much its economic relationships as its spirit of competition which pitted humans against one another, created class oppression, and destroyed sensitive individuals. Mankind needed no new economic order but rather a new ethical structure, a "religion of humanity," as she called it, borrowing a term from Auguste Comte and the Christian social gospel advocates of the late nineteenth century.

Yet her ethic of cooperation was often little more than a version of the romantic notion of cooperation among classes which had been a mainstay of conservative benevolent thought throughout the century. Like the ministers she elsewhere assailed, Cady Stanton thought it possible to teach the wealthy their responsibility to the poor according to "sound principles of political and domestic economy," which dictated that a healthy social order required a prosperous working class. While in England she praised the Salvation Army, kindergartens, and university settlements not only for educational and charitable work among the disadvantaged but also for teaching the well-to-do a new morality.

Such sentiments partook of the turn of the century utopian hope—apparent in both the social gospel and the settlement houses—that humanitarian self-sacrifice might become a new model for the well-to-do. But even in Cady Stanton's generally sensitive presentation, such ideas began to sound like naive rationalizations for wealth. Cady Stanton argued persuasively for the repeal of Sunday closing laws and for public Sunday recreation because that was the workers' only day off. But she revealed the limits of her understanding in the kind of recreational activities she advocated. She suggested that Sunday schools be expanded to further the teaching of morality and that the thousands of middle-class young women whose singing voices were the pride of their parents be encouraged to provide free afternoon concerts.

Conservatism tinged other areas of Cady Stanton's thought in the 1890s. Spencerian notions of inevitable struggle and progress led her to support American expansion on the grounds of the scientific and technological superiority of the United States. She even exonerated the government's violations of Indian rights. "What would have happened to this continent if left to the Indians?" she asked rhetorically, in response to criticisms that her position was racist. Moreover, she renewed her advocacy of the principle of educated suffrage, because, as she put it, the late-century European immigrants had "scarcely one element fitting them for the exercise of democratic principles." To her they represented "the evils of European monarchy and misrule transplanted to our shores." Even Anthony felt compelled to criticize Cady Stanton's resurrection of a position which she now found in violation of her friend's lifelong advocacy of individual rights.

That there were inconsistencies in Cady Stanton's thought

was not new: to the end she remained a polemicist as much as a philosopher, a journalist involved in commenting on a distinct series of events and issues rather than an analyst with a unified and disciplined point of view. But she continued to think of herself as a radical. In 1898 she challenged the NAWSA to give up its limited goal for the more comprehensive ideal of cooperation that would afford a way of remodeling "codes and constitutions, creeds, catechisms ... the curriculum of schools and colleges" to inspire "justice, liberty, and equality" in all relations of life, not just those involving men and women. In 1893 she declared her support of the populists and claimed that if the prohibitionists, populists, labor, and feminists would unite, they would have an electoral majority. But she did not extend support to Frances Willard who, in a later, radical phase of her own career, had undertaken such a mission.

Despite her interest in broad social issues in the 1890s, Cady Stanton's feminism remained as strong as ever. In England her closest relationships were with women moral reformers who reinforced her belief in woman's moral superiority. She reiterated views first expressed decades earlier when she wrote in 1900 that woman's moral power was the key to society's progress. "When the sexes reach a perfect equilibrium," she continued, "we shall have higher conditions in the state, the church, and the home." Nor had her utopianism diminished in these years. "There are great moral laws as fixed and universal as the laws of the material world," she wrote in 1900. "And there is a moral as well as material development going on all along the line, bringing the nations of the earth to a higher point of civilization." It was still important to her, as she neared the end of her life, that her own work be judged a success as well as a step toward assurance of the future attainment of feminist goals. "Progress," she declared, "is the law."

During the last years of her life, Cady Stanton lived in New York City with her son Robert, a lawyer, and her widowed daughter, Margaret, who, as did Harriot, fulfilled her feminist upbringing by becoming a professor of physical education at Columbia Teacher's College. All her sons, like their father, had gained law degrees, but only Theodore among the boys fulfilled her hopes that the children might carry on her reform work. Her eldest sons continued to disappoint her: Daniel made a fortune in the Louisiana Reconstruction government through shady financial manipulation and died in 1891; Henry was a corporation lawyer; Gerrit gained a minor reputation as a naturalist and then became a real estate broker on Long Island. After Henry Stanton's death in 1887, when Cady Stanton was seventy-two, she sold the Tenafly house. She always regretted having done so, for she now depended on others for a home.

She remained close to Susan Anthony, who unsuccessfully tried to persuade her friend to live with her in Rochester. In 1891, after her last trip to England, Cady Stanton visited Anthony, and the two of them, happiest when actively involved together, began a campaign to integrate the all-male University of Rochester. In addition, they sat for the massive tribute to the woman's movement which Adeline Johnson sculpted of them—and posthumously of Lucretia Mott—for the 1893 Chicago Columbian Centennial, now in the collection of statues in the national capitol. In 1894, reminiscent of old crusades, they worked together for a woman suffrage amendment before yet another New York State constitutional revision convention. Cady Stanton still wrote speeches for Anthony, elected president of the NAWSA after her own resignation.

Yet there was continuing tension in their relationship. Many of Cady Stanton's speeches during these years allude to her anger against Anthony, who was often allied with her opponents and who was critical of Cady Stanton's *Woman's Bible* and her autobiography, *Eighty Years and More.* Speaking at the 1890 celebration of Anthony's seventieth birthday, Cady Stanton termed their friendship one of "hard work and self-denial" in which they had been "thorns in the side of each other." Still they kept their disagreements private. The closest they came to open dispute was when they supported different candidates to succeed Anthony as president of the NAWSA in 1900. Anthony's close associate and biographer, Ida Husted Harper, wrote Cady Stanton criticizing her sternly for hurting Anthony by opposing her choice of a successor and for forgetting the many times that Anthony had engineered her election to the presidency. But Harper also indicated that Anthony herself never would have admitted such feelings to her friend. For her part, Cady Stanton also kept her feelings under control, writing to Lillie Devereux Blake, the unsuccessful candidate for NAWSA president, that both of them had been badly treated by "our younger coadjutors." In her own case they refused to read her letters and resolutions to woman suffrage conventions; they denounced *The Woman's Bible* and paid no attention to her autobiography. She nevertheless counseled Blake to adopt a philosophical attitude, that sentiments of discontent, anger, and revenge accomplished little.

By and large Cady Stanton was content during the last years of her life. Decades before she had conquered her youthful emotionalism and her tendency to depression. Indeed, her daughter Margaret described Cady Stanton's old age in New York City as radiant. She was full of fun. As always she loved pranks and parties, especially when she played and sang the songs of her youth. Her grandchildren adored her, for she had retained her gift of storytelling and her love of children's games. They called her "Queen Mother." Poor health, however, increasingly troubled her in the 1890s. She found travel difficult and rarely attended public functions outside New York City. By 1900 her eyesight began to fail; by the time of her death she was totally blind. She spent her time with family and close friends and, as long as she could, in reading and writing. She published an article in the *New York American,* reiterating her liberal views on divorce, one week before her death and had undertaken negotiations to publish an edition of her speeches, a project never brought to fruition.

By family legend, Cady Stanton took her own life. According to her great-granddaughter, as her eyesight and health began to fail, she decided that she would choose to live no longer when she felt her usefulness was ending. By this account, she persuaded her physician—a woman and fellow feminist—to give her an overdose of drugs when she asked for it. Like Charlotte Perkins Gilman, who took her own life in 1935 when the cancer from which she suffered became severe, Cady Stanton wanted to have the same control over her death that she had achieved over her life. Yet the story itself may be an elaboration, in the passage of decades, of a remark that Cady Stanton made to her doctor the day before her death. In Harriot Stanton Blatch's recorded account, Cady Stanton asked to be "speeded on to heaven" if she could no longer work.

Whatever occurred, the events surrounding Cady Stanton's death, like many other deathbed scenes, reveal much about her character. When the end appeared near, she was calm and accepting. Several hours before her death, on October 26, 1902, she asked her daughters to help dress her and arrange her hair—the thickness and color of which she had always been proud. It was as though she were preparing, as she so often had done, to go to a party or to give a speech. Soon, she stood, erect, her hands on a table supporting her, and she remained so for seven or eight minutes. "I think," wrote Blatch, "she was mentally making an address." Then she sat down at the table and fell asleep. Two hours later she died.

A Note on the Sources

WITH THE exception of Alma Lutz, *Created Equal: A Biography of Elizabeth Cady Stanton* (New York: John Day, 1940), no scholarly biography of Cady Stanton has yet been written. Cady Stanton's autobiography, *Eighty Years and More: Reminiscences, 1815–1897* (New York: T. Fisher Unwin, 1898), is an indispensable beginning. *History of Woman Suffrage*, Vols. 1–3, ed. Elizabeth Cady Stanton, Susan B. Anthony, and Matilda Jocelyn Gage (New York: Fowler and Wells, 1881 and 1882; Rochester, N.Y.: Susan B. Anthony, 1886); Vol. 4, ed. Susan B. Anthony and Ida Husted Harper (Rochester: Susan B. Anthony, 1886) offers a wealth of biographical data and information on the woman's movement. Theodore Stanton and Harriot Stanton Blatch eds., *Elizabeth Cady Stanton as Revealed in Her Letters, Diary, and Reminiscences*, 2 vols. (New York: Harper and Bros., 1922), is also invaluable, although Blatch and Stanton edited the letters in accordance with their personal tastes and give no indication of what they have omitted. Perhaps the most insightful account of Cady Stanton's life was written by her friend, Laura Curtis Bullard, in Elizabeth Stuart Phelps et al., eds., *Our Famous Women* (Hartford: Hartford Publishing, 1888). There is also material in Harriot Stanton Blatch and Alma Lutz, *Challenging Years: The Memoirs of Harriot Stanton Blatch* (New York: Putnam's, 1940). I disagree with Judith Nies, *Seven Women: Portraits from the American Radical Tradition* (New York: Viking, 1977), that Cady Stanton had excellent political skills, and with Alice S. Rossi, ed., *The Feminist Papers: From Adams to Beauvoir* (New York: Columbia, 1973), that Cady Stanton suffered from status discontent.

Given the paucity of published material on Cady Stanton, I have consulted numerous manuscript collections, including the Andrew Dickson White Papers at Cornell University; the Theodore Stanton Collection of Elizabeth Cady Stanton Papers at Douglass College of Rutgers University; the Elizabeth Boynton Harbert Papers at the Henry E. Huntington Library; the Blackwell Family, Elizabeth Cady Stanton, Susan B. Anthony, and Olivia Hall Papers, and the Susan B. Anthony Scrapbooks at the Library of Congress; the Political Equality

Club of Minnesota Papers at the Minnesota Historical Society; the Lillie Devereux Blake Papers at the Missouri Historical Society; the Elizabeth Smith Miller and Susan B. Anthony Papers at the New York Public Library; the Susan B. Anthony, Olympia Brown, Matilda J. Gage, Blackwell Family, Harriet Robinson, Woman's Rights, and Alma Lutz Papers at the Schlesinger Library of Radcliffe College; the miscellaneous Stanton Clippings at the Seneca Falls Historical Society; the Susan B. Anthony, Garrison Family, Carpenter, and Woman's Rights Papers at the Sophia Smith Collection of Smith College; the Victoria Woodhull papers at Southern Illinois University; the Susan B. Anthony Papers at the University of Rochester; the Gerrit Smith Papers at the University of Syracuse; the Elizabeth Cady Stanton and Alma Lutz Papers at Vassar College; and the Mathilde Franziska Anneke Papers at the Wisconsin Historical Society.

I have had to exert caution in using Cady Stanton's voluminous papers because of her vagueness in noting dates. For instance, she cites 1832 and 1833 in varying instances as the date of her graduation from Emma Willard; and in an unpublished memoir in the Minnesota Historical Society she incorrectly dates her 1854 appearance before the New York State legislature as 1848. Moreover, she disliked clutter and regularly discarded correspondence, destroying, for example, most of the letters that Susan Anthony wrote her.

In addition to her autobiography and the suffrage history, which includes many of her speeches, Cady Stanton's writings are to be found in many newspapers and journals of the period, including *The Lily*, 1849–58; *The Una*, 1853–55; *The Revolution*, 1868–72; *The National Citizen and Ballot Box*, 1876–81. In addition, one can consult *The Arena* (March 1890; June 1897); *The Critic* (March 28, 1896); *The Forum* (April 1886); *The Nation* (Oct. 1885); *The North American Review* (Dec. 1882; May 1885; Dec. 1900); *The Open Court* (Oct. 12, 1893); *The Westminster Review* (July-Dec. 1893). See also *The Woman's Bible* (New York: European, 1895).

Biographies exist for most of Cady Stanton's woman's rights friends and associates, although many of these works lack scholarly precision and are out of date. Among the most rewarding are several studies of Susan Anthony, including Alma Lutz, *Susan B. Anthony: Rebel, Crusader, Humanitarian* (Boston: Beacon, 1959); Katharine Anthony, *Susan B. Anthony: Her Personal History and Her Era* (New York: Russell and Russell, 1954); and Ida Husted Harper, *The Life of Susan B. Anthony*, 3 vols. (Indianapolis: Hollenbeck, 1908), written by

Harper with Anthony's assistance—after which Anthony destroyed many of her papers. In addition, one can benefit from consulting Elinor Rice Hays, *Morning Star: A Biography of Lucy Stone* (New York: Harcourt, Brace, 1961); Anna Davis Hallowell, ed., *James and Lucretia Mott: Life and Letters* (Boston: Houghton Mifflin, 1884); and especially Gerda Lerner, *The Grimké Sisters from South Carolina: Rebels Against Slavery* (Boston: Houghton Mifflin, 1967). Arthur Rice, "Henry B. Stanton as a Political Abolitionist" (Ph.D. diss., Columbia Teachers College, 1968) is of inestimable value in understanding Henry Stanton, whose own autobiography, *Random Recollections* (New York: Harper and Bros., 1887), is unrevealing.

General works on the woman's movement and the nineteenth-century background include Eleanor Flexner, *Century of Struggle* (Cambridge, Mass.: Harvard, 1959); Robert Riegel, *American Feminists* (Lawrence: University of Kansas, 1963); and Andrew Sinclair, *The Better Half: The Emancipation of the American Woman* (New York: Harper and Row, 1965). Especially insightful are Ross Evans Paulson, *Women's Suffrage and Prohibition: A Comparative Study of Equality and Social Control* (Glenview, Ill.: Scott, Foresman, 1973), and Carroll Smith-Rosenberg, "The Female World of Love and Ritual: Relations Between Women in Nineteenth-Century America," *Signs: Journal of Women in Culture and Society* 1 (Autumn 1975), 1–25. Edward T. James et al., eds., *Notable American Women* (Cambridge, Mass.: Harvard, 1971), is indispensable. I disagree with the argument of Barbara J. Berg, *The Remembered Gate: Origins of American Feminism: The Woman and the City, 1800–1860* (New York: Oxford, 1978), that nineteenth-century feminism was particularly an urban phenomenon.

Chapter I

For information on Johnstown, I have consulted local histories and gazetteers, including J. Disturnell, *A Gazetteer of the State of New York* (New York: C. Van Benthuysen, 1843); T. Wood Clarke, *Bloody Mohawk* (New York: Macmillan, 1940); and Washington Frothingham, *History of Montgomery and Fulton Counties* (Syracuse: D. Mason, 1892). For the religious background, Whitney R. Cross, *The Burned-Over District: The Social and Intellectual History of Enthusiastic Religion in Western New York, 1800–1850* (Ithaca: Cornell, 1950), and Robert Hastings Nichols, *Presbyterianism in New York State* (Philadelphia: Westminster, 1963), are helpful, as is Philip Greven, *The Protestant Temperament:*

Patterns of Child-Rearing, Religious Experience, and the Self in Early America (New York: Knopf, 1977), for the Cadys' child rearing practices. However, Cady Stanton's experience does not validate his separation of evangelical, moderate, and genteel child rearing modes. Biographical material on Daniel Cady is contained in Henry Stanton, "Daniel Cady," in Oliver Barbour, ed., *New York Supreme Court: Reports of Cases* (Albany: W. C. Little, 1848–58), app., and Peyton Miller, *A Group of Great Lawyers of Columbia County, New York* (N. P., 1904). For the Livingston background, see Joan Gordon, "The Livingstons of New York, 1675–1860: Kinship and Class" (Ph.D. diss., Columbia, 1959). On homeopathy, see Martin Kaufman, *Homeopathy in America: The Rise and Fall of a Medical Heresy* (Baltimore: Johns Hopkins, 1971), and on phrenology, John D. Davies, *Phrenology, Fad and Science: A Nineteenth-Century American Crusade* (New Haven: Yale, 1955). George Combe's major work is *The Constitution of Man Considered in Relation to External Objects* (New York: Wells, 1828); Amelia Willard's lectures were published as *Lectures to Young Ladies* (New York: Leavitt, Lord, 1836). On Gerrit Smith and Peterboro, see Ralph Volney Harlow, *Gerrit Smith: Philanthropist and Reformer* (New York: Henry Holt, 1939), and on Emma Willard, Anne Firor Scott, "What, Then, Is the American: The New Woman," *Journal of American History* 65 (Dec. 1978), 679–703. Important genealogical information is contained in Henry Stiles, *History of Ancient Windsor, Connecticut* (Albany: J. Munsell, 1863), and in William Stanton, *A Record, Genealogical and Biographical, Statistical, of Thomas Stanton, of Connecticut and His Descendants* (Albany: John Munsell's Sons, 1891). Lois Hoffman, "Early Childhood Experiences and Women's Achievement Motives," in Sandra Schwartz Tangri, Martha T. Mednick, and Lois W. Hoffman, eds., *Women and Achievement: Social and Motivational Analyses* (Washington, D.C.: Hemisphere, 1975), concludes that maternal rejection is a positive stimulus to daughters of homebound women in allowing them to reject their mother's domestic role.

Chapter II

On reform in general in early nineteenth-century America, see Ronald G. Walters, *American Reformers, 1815–1860* (New York: Hill and Wang, 1978), and Lois W. Banner, "Religious Benevolence as Social Control: A Critique of an Interpretation," *Journal of American History* 60 (June 1973), 23–41. On abolitionism, for which the sources are voluminous, James Brewer Stewart, *Holy Warriors: The Abolitionists and American Slavery* (New York: Hill and Wang, 1976), and Gerald

Sorin, *Abolitionism: A New Perspective* (New York: Greenwood, 1972), survey recent scholarship. My interpretation of Garrisonianism has been influenced by John L. Thomas, *The Liberator: William Lloyd Garrison* (Boston: Little, Brown, 1963); Aileen Kraditor, *Means and Ends in American Abolitionism* (New York: Vintage, 1969); and Bertram Wyatt-Brown, "William Lloyd Garrison and Antislavery Unity: A Reappraisal," *Civil War History* 13 (March 1967), 5–24. Lucretia Mott's diary has been published as Frederick B. Tolles, ed., *Slavery and "the Woman Question": Lucretia Mott's Diary of Her Visit to Great Britain to Attend the World's Antislavery Convention of 1840* (Haverford, Pa.: Friends Historical Assn., 1952). The most recent analyses of the relationship between abolitionism and woman's rights include Blanche Glassman Hersh, *The Slavery of Sex: Feminist-Abolitionists in America* (Urbana: Illinois University, 1978); Keith Melder, *Beginnings of Sisterhood: The American Woman's Rights Movement, 1800–1850* (New York: Schocken, 1977); and Ellen DuBois, *Feminism and Suffrage: The Emergence of an Independent Women's Movement in America, 1848–1869* (Ithaca: Cornell, 1978).

Andrew Combe's work is *A Treatise on the Physiological and Moral Management of Infancy* (Philadelphia: Carey & Hart, 1840).

In understanding the crises of Cady Stanton's emotional life, I have been particularly influenced by the work of Erik H. Erikson, especially by *Life History and the Historical Moment* (New York: Norton, 1975).

Chapter III

Material on Seneca Falls can be found in *Centennial Volume of Papers of the Seneca Falls Historical Society* (Seneca Falls: Seneca Falls Historical Society, 1948), and in Robert S. Riegel, ed., "Woman's Rights and Other Reforms at Seneca Falls: A Contemporary View," *New York History* 46 (Jan. 1965), 41–59. On temperance see John Krout, *Origins of Prohibition* (New York: Knopf, 1925), and Amelia Bloomer, *Life and Writings,* ed. Dexter Bloomer (Boston: Arena, 1895). On dress reform see Robert S. Riegel, "Women's Clothes and Women's Rights," *American Quarterly* 15 (Fall 1963), 390–401; on divorce reform, see Nelson Manfred Blake, *The Road to Reno: A History of Divorce in the United States* (New York: Macmillan, 1962).

The date of Cady Stanton's meeting with Anthony is unclear. I have followed previous biographers of these women by citing it as 1851. Amelia Bloomer, however, remembered it as 1850.

Chapter IV

For the philosophical background of Cady Stanton's feminism, I have found especially helpful Richmond Laurin Hawkins, *Positivism in the United States* (Cambridge, Mass.: Harvard, 1938); Richard Hofstadter, *Social Darwinism in American Thought* (Philadelphia: University of Pennsylvania, 1944); Davies on phrenology (see p. 252); Elizabeth Fee, "The Sexual Politics of Victorian Social Anthropology," in Mary S. Hartman and Lois W. Banner, eds., *Clio's Consciousness Raised: New Perspectives on the History of Women* (New York: Harper and Row, 1974); Linda Kerber, "The Republican Mother: Women and the Enlightenment—An American Perspective," *American Quarterly* 28 (Summer 1976), 187–205; Frank E. Manuel, *The Prophets of Paris* (Cambridge, Mass: Harvard, 1962); and John L. Thomas, "Romantic Reform in America, 1815–1865," *American Quarterly* 17 (Winter 1965), 656–681. Susan Phinney Conrad, *Perish the Thought: Intellectual Women in Modern America, 1830–1860* (New York: Oxford, 1976), offers some interesting glosses, although her argument that feminism is an outgrowth of romanticism is simplistic. Linda Gordon, *Woman's Body, Woman's Right: A Social History of Birth Control in America* (New York: Grossman, 1976), and James Mohr, *Abortion in America: The Origins and Evolution of National Policy, 1800–1900* (New York: Oxford, 1978), are exemplary studies of their subjects.

Chapter V

Among the many analyses of Reconstruction politics, James McPherson's excellent study, *The Struggle for Equality: Abolitionists and the Negro in the Civil War and Reconstruction* (Princeton: Princeton Univ., 1964), is the most useful for the Reconstruction amendments. His "Abolitionists, Woman Suffrage, and the Negro," *Mid-America* 47 (1965), 40–46, offers some additional information. On the Workingwoman's Association and the Hester Vaughan trial, Ellen DuBois, *Feminism and Suffrage,* is insightful, although my analysis of these episodes differs from hers. David Pivar has reconstructed the complex history of the social purity movement in *Purity Crusade: Sexual Morality and Social Control* (Westport, Conn: Greenwood, 1973).

For information on New York City I have used Matthew Hale Smith, *Sunshine and Shadow in New York* (Hartford: J. B. Burr, 1868), and George Ellington, *Women of New York* (New York: New York Book, 1869).

Chapter VI

Robert S. Riegel interprets the 1869 division in "Split of the Feminist Movement in 1869," *Mississippi Valley Historical Review* 49 (Dec. 1962), 485–496, as the result of personality clashes. I am indebted to Suzanne Desan, "The 1869 Split in the Woman's Movement," a Junior Paper written at Princeton University in 1977 under my direction, for helping me to see the errors in his analysis. On the lyceum see Carl Bode, *The American Lyceum: Town Meeting of the Mind* (New York: Oxford, 1956). Daniel Scott Smith, "Family Limitation, Sexual Control, and Domestic Feminism," in Hartman and Banner, *Clio's Consciousness Raised*, offers data on nineteenth-century birth control. Aside from Madeleine Stern, *The Victoria Woodhull Reader* (Weston, Mass: M & S, 1974), a compilation of speeches and writings, there is no judicious study of Victoria Woodhull, although one might consult Joanna Johnston, *Mrs. Satan: The Incredible Saga of Victoria C. Woodhull* (New York: Putnam's, 1967). For Alexandra Gripenberg on Cady Stanton see *A Half Year in the United States,* ed. and trans. Ernest J. Moyne (Newark: University of Deleware, 1954).

Chapter VII

The Beecher-Tilton trial still awaits its historian, although Robert Shaplen, *Free Love and Heavenly Sinners: The Story of the Great Henry Ward Beecher Scandal* (New York: Knopf, 1954), is a well-reasoned analysis, and Paxton Hibben, *Henry Ward Beecher: An American Portrait* (New York: Doran, 1927), remains an exemplary biography. On the Beecher family, see Marie Caskey, *Chariot of Fire: Religion and the Beecher Family* (New Haven: Yale, 1978). For the post-Civil War woman suffrage movement, I have used in particular Lois Merk, "Massachusetts and the Woman Suffrage Movement" (Ph.D. diss., Radcliffe College, 1961). Two doctoral dissertations provide the most recent studies of the Women's Christian Temperance Union and of the woman's clubs. See Janet Zollinger Giele, "Social Change in the Feminine Role: A Comparison of Woman's Suffrage and Woman's Temperance, 1870–1920" (Ph.D. diss., Radcliffe College, 1961), and Karen J. Blair, "The Clubwoman as Feminist: The Woman's Culture Club Movement in the United States, 1868–1914" (Ph.D. diss., State University of New York at Buffalo, 1976). On the woman's clubs, Jennie C. Croly, *The History of the Women's Club Movement* (New York: Allen, 1898), is still valuable.

On Frances Willard, see Mary Earhart, *Frances Willard: From Prayers to Politics* (Chicago: University of Chicago, 1944); on the International Council of Women, see Edith Hurwitz, "The International Sisterhood," in Renate Bridenthal and Claudia Koontz, eds., *Becoming Visible: Women in European History* (Boston: Houghton Mifflin, 1977), and on woman's issues in the late nineteenth century, see the first chapter of Lois W. Banner, *Women in Modern America: A Brief History* (New York: Harcourt, Brace, 1974).

Chapter VIII

Cady Stanton's analysis of religion in nineteenth-century America differs substantially from the thesis advanced by a number of historians, including Barbara Welter, "The Feminization of American Religion: 1800–1860," in Banner and Hartman, *Clio's Consciousness Raised,* and Ann Douglas, *The Feminization of American Culture* (New York: Knopf, 1977), that American religion was feminized. As business and politics increasingly captured men's interest in a modernizing America, so the argument goes, women became the majority of church members. Accordingly, rigorous Puritan creeds and ceremonies were softened and sentimentalized, and the status of ministers presumably declined.

Welter's and Douglas's studies both deal with the early part of the century; for the post-Civil War period no study exists. I have relied on Ada C. Bowles, "Women in the Ministry," in Annie Nathan Meyer, ed., *Woman's Work in America* (New York: Henry Holt, 1891); R. Pierce Beaver, *All Love's Excelling: American Protestant Women in World Missions* (Grand Rapids, Mich.: Eerdmans, 1968); and Margaret Meier, "Some Themes in the History of American Women and Religion in Late-Nineteenth Century," a Senior Thesis completed at Princeton University in 1978 under my direction. On the social gospel, see William R. Hutchison, *The Modernist Impulse in American Protestantism* (Cambridge, Mass.: Harvard, 1976); on Fabianism, see Norman MacKenzie and Jeanne MacKenzie, *The Fabians* (New York: Simon and Schuster, 1977); and on cooperation, see Herbert B. Adams, *History of Cooperation in the United States* (Baltimore: Johns Hopkins, 1888). For the English background, Herman Ausubel, *In Hard Times: Reformers Among the Late Victorians* (New York: Columbia, 1960), is excellent.

Recent work on women and American religion can be found in the Winter 1978 issue of the *American Quarterly,* ed. Janet Wilson James.

Index

love, views on, 112,
114–115; *History of Woman
Suffrage,* 146–149, 157;
homeopathy, interest in,
14, 50; House of
Representatives, campaign
for, 93; husband,
relationship with, 25,
32–38; Independence Hall
protest, role in, 138–139;
individualism of, 74–76;
international woman's
organization, interest in,
149–152; lyceum tours of,
110–111, 121–125;
marriage, views on, 36,
80–84, 118; mother,
relationship with, 4, 10;
National Woman Suffrage
Association, foundation of
and participation in, 113,
130, 138–145, 154; penal
reform, interest in, 6, 165;
political style of, 44–46,
59, 88–89; prostitution,
views on, 73, 96; racial
attitudes of, 74, 97, 169;
religious experience of, 13,
30, 49; sexuality, attitude
toward, 35, 82–83, 114;
temperance, interest in, 29,
54–55, 62–64; utopianism
of, 30, 85–88, 166–169;
Woman's Bible, 161–165;
Woman's Rights
Convention, Seneca Falls
(1848), 39–42, 46–47;
woman suffrage, views on,
42–44, 71, 100; Woodhull,
involvement with, 125–131;

working class, attitude
toward, 74, 106, 166,
168–169; writings of, 70
Catt, Carrie Chapman, 164–165
Channing, William Henry, 155
Chicago World's Fair
(Columbian Centennial),
162, 171
Coeducation, Cady Stanton's
views on, 12, 78
Colby, Clara Berwick, 160
Combe, Andrew, 28
Combe, George, 13–14
Communitarianism, 29–30,
87–88, 166–167
Comstock, Anthony, 107, 135,
138, 143
Comte, Auguste, 86, 166, 168
Conway, Moncure, 166
Cooperative movement,
167–169

Davis, Paulina Wright, 29,
135
Democratic party, 33, 95, 100,
132
Dickinson, Mary Lowes, 153
Divorce reform, 61–62, 66,
79–81
Douglass, Frederick, 30, 42, 44,
113, 145
Dress reform, 35, 55–57

Eaton, Daniel, 9, 47, 68
Emancipation Proclamation, 93,
94
Emerson, Ralph Waldo, 29, 75,
110
Equal Rights party, 129, 130
Eugenics, 81–82